MW01514840

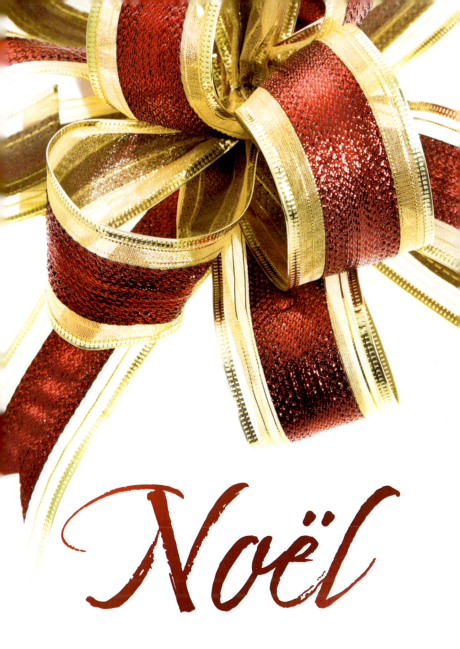

Noël

AN ADVENT DEVOTIONAL

Denise Glenn

Permissions:
Kardo Ministries
Houston, TX, USA
713-849-9335 / 888-272-6972
info@kardo.org

Scan QR code to order additional copies

Cover and book design by Kristan King

Printed in the United States of America

"Experience a life-transforming Advent with NOEL! Denise combines the Old Testament with the Gospels, bringing the Christmas Story to a new level of personal intimacy. This devotional will ignite your soul and prepare your heart for the true meaning of Christmas!"
Mary Ann Bridgwater, President, Pray the Word Ministries

"I love how this devotional not only tells the Christmas story through the eyes of Mary and Joseph but gives the Gospel message as well. "O Come Let Us Adore HIM" this Christmas season in reading this devotional. It's a wonderful gift for the entire family!"
F.C., Memphis, Tennessee

"Reading "Noel" has brought me great joy. Denise beautifully weaves Jewish traditions into the story of young Mary, expressing her deep faith and the emotions of her situation to make it come alive for us. The devotionals feel like they were written by God Himself.
L.B., Houston, Texas

"I highly recommend reading the Advent devotional, "Noel," a 31-day devotional that's perfect for the Christmas season. Each day starts with a short and powerful prayer, followed by a relatable Biblical story that's easy to understand. The daily message is backed up with scriptures and ends with a practical tip that can change your life."
J.P., Tulsa, Oklahoma

Other Books by Denise Glenn

Wisdom for Mothers

Freedom for Mothers

Restore My Heart

Keeping the Secrets of Jesus

Fan the Flame

Winter Season

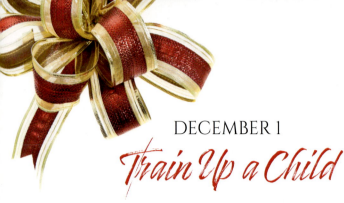

DECEMBER 1

Train Up a Child

Heavenly Father, as I embark on another season of celebrating Your birth, teach me fresh and new truths from Your Word. Speak into my life, Lord. In Jesus' name. Amen.

She was only eleven, but she already knew a lot about the Torah and the writings of Solomon. Her father had seen to Mary's education in the sacred writings. He wanted both his sons and daughters to be schooled in the eternal truths passed down through the generations of the children of Israel. Mary was his firstborn daughter and his pride and joy. Beautiful on the inside and out, there was a special light in her eyes. He began teaching her all of the fantastic stories of Abraham, Isaac, and Jacob when she was five. She could recite by heart the accounts of Adam and Eve and Noah before her sixth birthday. Mary was bright but not conceited and beautiful but not haughty. She was quiet, curious, a hard worker and fun-loving. Her obedience brought great joy to both her mother and her father.

But now it was time to prepare Mary for her coming-of-age celebration, later in history, to become the Bat Mitzvah. (While boys celebrate Bar Mitzvah at 13, girls are ceremonially brought through the rite of passage from childhood to adulthood in the Jewish community at 12. Roughly coinciding with puberty, the ceremony, usually held on the Sabbath after their birthday of eligible age, was a community event.) In her little village, this celebration would be at home, not in the synagogue. She was a girl from a poor family. Her special day would be shared with their closest relatives and neighbors.

Mary couldn't wait for the Shabbat following her twelfth birthday. On this special Friday night, she would be allowed to light the Shabbat candles and say the blessing to begin the holy night for the family gathered around the table. After this night, she would be responsible for keeping all of the commandments and laws of her people and would be recognized as an adult woman in the community. She took a deep breath. She thought to herself, "Am I ready for that? I have so much to learn!" She was thankful her father and mother were law-abiding believers in Yahweh and obeyed His commands as stated in Deuteronomy. Because of their faithfulness, she would be ready for her big day.

Deuteronomy 6:4-7

"Hear, O Israel: The LORD our God, the LORD is one. You shall love the LORD your God with all your heart and with all your soul and with all your might. And these words that I command you today shall be on your heart. You shall teach them diligently to your children, and shall talk of them when you sit in your house, and when you walk by the way, and when you lie down, and when you rise."

Preparing My Heart for Christmas

Encourage the children of the family to play with the Nativity set by placing it within reach. Ask them to rearrange the figures and explain why they think Mary, Joseph, Baby Jesus, the shepherds, and wise men should be placed there. Use this opportunity to discuss the story of Jesus' birth and fill in additional details they might still need to learn.

DECEMBER 2

The Beauty of Womanhood

Father in heaven, please pour Your love, joy, peace, and patience
through me to my family this season. In Jesus' name. Amen.

Aunt Rachel, the sister of Mary's mother, was chosen to train her young niece. Rachel loved teaching, and she was good at it. She made it interesting and fun but didn't skirt around a commandment because it was uncomfortable. No, Rachel was diligent in teaching her young charges everything commanded by God for women. Rachel was convinced that girls should be trained to be wives before they entered puberty. Before any handsome boy turned their heads, Rachel wanted them to know the duties and responsibilities, the joys and the sorrows of being married.

The girls in her family would be trained to be faithful, caring, diligent, and hard-working wives. They would be good mothers, good cooks, and good household managers. They would be taught to meet their husband's needs and respect them with their words, attitudes, and actions. They would be taught to be respectful, submissive wives, but not passive. The girls had to have a backbone and speak up with their opinions. Their husbands would need and reply upon their intelligent contributions regarding how the family was run, but they would learn to allow their husbands the final say. This was Yahweh's plan for marriage, and no girl in her charge would enter marriage ignorant of the commandments designed to protect women. The young women she taught would be prepared to cut a marriage covenant that would last a lifetime.

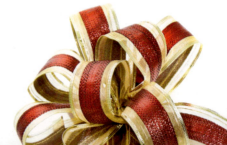

Today, they would begin with her favorite passage from King Solomon's writing. "Mary," she called as she entered the small courtyard. "Mary, it's time to stop playing with your brothers and sisters and join me inside. We have an important lesson in a beautiful passage from the wisest man who ever lived. If you listen to and obey his wisdom, your life as a Jewish woman, wife, and mother will be blessed. Come now. Let's settle down and read together."

Proverbs 31:10-12, 25-30 (KJV)

Who can find a virtuous woman? For her price is far above rubies. The heart of her husband does safely trust in her so that he shall have no need of spoil. She will do him good and not evil all the days of her life.

Strength and dignity are her clothing, and she laughs at the time to come. She opens her mouth with wisdom, and the teaching of kindness is on her tongue. She looks well to the ways of her household and does not eat the bread of idleness. Her children rise up and call her blessed; her husband also and he praises her: "Many women have done excellently, but you surpass them all." Charm is deceitful, and beauty is vain, but a woman who fears the Lord is to be praised.

Preparing My Heart for Christmas

Create simple family traditions. You might prepare an Advent wreath and light the candles each Sunday leading up to Christmas. If your family is musical, go Christmas caroling. Include only traditions that bring you joy, not stress!

DECEMBER 3
Lessons on Marriage

Lord, thank You for keeping Your promises to me. Now, please give me the courage and strength to keep my promises to those in my family. In Jesus' name, I pray. Amen.

———◦◉◦———

Mary was a good student of the Torah. While Temple law forbade her from studying in the synagogue with boys her age, she had diligent tutors in her father, mother, and aunts to prepare her to be a wife. There were many things to learn before she joined the Jewish community on her twelfth birthday. They prepared her for the day a man would choose her to be his son's wife. Right now, that seemed in the distant future. But marrying young was common in their village, and she had to be prepared for it any time after she went through the religious rite of passage and her body bloomed into womanhood.

Today's lesson was on covenant and what it meant to promise herself to a man for the rest of her life. Her eyes widened as Auntie Rachel explained the seriousness of cutting covenant with a man who would be her husband. This permanent, binding agreement between two individuals was not to be broken during one's lifetime.

Mary knew the sacredness of covenant cutting. It was part of Jewish culture that went all the way back to God's covenant promises to Abraham and ran through their history, including Jonathan's covenant with David. She knew that to break a covenant promise deserved death. Her decision to enter a covenant betrothal with her future husband would be the most serious pledge of her life—second only to her promise to love God with all of her heart, soul, and mind. Even at eleven, Mary pondered these things in her heart.

She spent some time alone after the lesson. What an important step she would take one day! God would ask her to join a covenant relationship with her husband that would last until her last breath.

I Samuel 18: 3-4

Then Jonathan made a covenant with David because he loved him as his own soul. And Jonathan stripped himself of the robe that was on him and gave it to David, and his armor, and even his sword and his bow and his belt.

Preparing My Heart for Christmas

This Christmas season and beyond, let your actions speak louder than words by being true to your commitments to your loved ones, colleagues, and church. Whether showing up on time for a family gathering or following through on a project at work, your integrity and dependability will inspire trust and respect in those around you. Embrace the opportunity to be a reliable and trustworthy person in all aspects of your life, and let your faithfulness shine through.

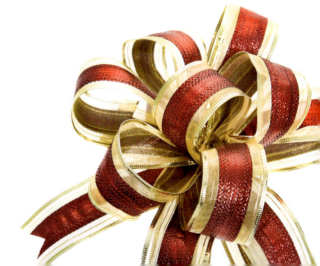

Warnings for a Bride

Lord Jesus, open the eyes of my heart and flood them with light.
During this Christmas season, please show me how to walk in the
light and away from darkness in my actions and attitudes.
In Jesus' holy name, I pray. Amen.

><><><

Mary's mother, Martha, was a no-nonsense kind of woman. She managed a large household of children, made and sold garments in the village, and provided food for her family and the young maids who helped her run the home. Her husband trusted her completely with the organization of their bustling family.

Martha was not too busy to teach her girls the wonder and the warnings about marriage. The Torah was very clear about what happens when a marriage breaks down. If a husband finds that his betrothed has been unfaithful to him, the law declares her punishment is her death!

So, Martha schooled her girls on the sacredness of their bodies, the reason their father was so protective about their relationships with boys, and why they were to remain virgins until their wedding night. The night they married was to be a joyous coming together of two virgins. In the privacy of her bedroom with the girls gathered on her bed, Martha wanted her daughters to know that sexual union in marriage was the glue to bind them to their husbands in life-long love. It was God's design to bring forth children into a home where the mother and father loved each other in a deeply committed covenant marriage. Mary pondered these lessons as she knew they were of utmost importance and could save not only her future marriage but her life!

Deuteronomy 22:13-21

If any man takes a wife and goes in to her and then hates her and accuses her of misconduct and brings a bad name upon her, saying, 'I took this woman, and when I came near her, I did not find in her evidence of virginity,' then the father of the young woman and her mother shall take and bring out the evidence of her virginity to the elders of the city in the gate. And the father of the young woman shall say to the elders, 'I gave my daughter to this man to marry, and he hates her; and behold, he has accused her of misconduct, saying, "I did not find in your daughter evidence of virginity." And yet this is the evidence of my daughter's virginity.' And they shall spread the cloak before the elders of the city.

Then the elders of that city shall take the man and whip him, and they shall fine him a hundred shekels of silver and give them to the father of the young woman, because he has brought a bad name upon a virgin of Israel. And she shall be his wife. He may not divorce her all his days. But if the thing is true, that evidence of virginity was not found in the young woman, then they shall bring out the young woman to the door of her father's house, and the men of her city shall stone her to death with stones, because she has done an outrageous thing in Israel by whoring in her father's house. So you shall purge the evil from your midst.

Preparing My Heart for Christmas

Spend a few moments today asking God to purify your heart. If He brings anything to mind that you must confess and ask for forgiveness, take care of it before going to bed tonight. You'll sleep in heavenly peace.

DECEMBER 5

Love Song

Lord, here is my heart. Take it and use me as You will. Mold and shape me as a potter shapes the clay. I offer myself to You. In Jesus' holy name, I pray. Amen.

No one really understood Mary. She kept her feelings to herself; even as a young girl of eleven, she was a ponderer. But inside her heart, she sensed God had a plan for her life. She was to do something for God, but who knew what that would be? She turned these thoughts over and over in her mind.

One day, Aunt Rachel came to the house unannounced, which was not unusual, and drew Mary aside. "Mary, dear, let's go for a walk." With a look to Martha for approval and receiving a nod, Rachel and Mary grabbed their shawls and walked out into the sunlight. Mary loved to get out of the house and step outside the village into the countryside nearby. The air was sweeter, the sky seemed bluer, and the birds sang louder.

Mary drank it all in as they walked together in silence. When they had gone a long distance, Rachel suggested they stop for a rest and sit on a rock. Mary turned her face to the sun to absorb the warmth. Aunt Rachel spoke softly, "Mary, today's lesson is from a special book in Scripture. Today, we will read from the Song of Songs, written by King Solomon. This wise man wrote a love story more like a love poem. You are old enough to read, study, and prepare your heart for marriage to a man from our synagogue. It will take some years before you are ready to be wed, but it takes time to learn what it takes to receive the love of a man the way we are instructed."

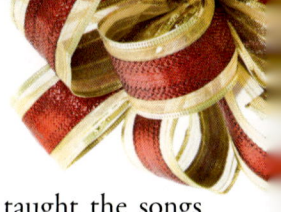

"Mary, all of the girls approaching puberty are taught the songs of Solomon. From them, you will learn how lovers speak to one another and how to receive compliments from your future husband. You should be anticipating your betrothal someday soon after the onset of puberty. God has a wonderful plan for your life and your marriage. That plan will be revealed to you on the right day and at the right time."

Song of Solomon 1:2-4, 13-16

Let him kiss me with the kisses of his mouth! For your love is better than wine; Your anointing oils are fragrant; your name is oil poured out; therefore virgins love you. Draw me after you; let us run. The king has brought me into his chambers.

My beloved is to me a sachet of myrrh that lies between my breasts. My beloved is to me a cluster of henna blossoms in the vineyards of Engedi. Behold, you are beautiful, my love; behold, you are beautiful; your eyes are doves. Behold, you are beautiful, my beloved, truly delightful.

Preparing My Heart for Christmas

As the Christmas season approaches, consider creating a new worship playlist on your device to celebrate the birth of Jesus. Look for beautiful renditions of classic hymns like "Silent Night" and "O Come Let Us Adore Him" that will inspire you to worship the Lord and reflect on the true meaning of Christmas. Fill your playlist with songs that bring you joy and peace, and use it to connect with God during this special time of year.

The Lineage of Messiah

Immanuel, God with us, Lord Jesus, holy one of God, I worship You.
Thank You that You came to love and to save us.
Lord, how glorious is your name, Amen.

—◦◦◦—

Mary's father carefully taught his children the prophecies from the scrolls. Over and over, they asked for their favorites as they sat around Heli's knee. "Please, Father, read Isaiah again. I like to hear the one about how the Messiah will come. It's like a fairy tale, hard to believe, yet we know it is true because it is in the sacred scroll." Heli gathered the children close to his side and closed his eyes as he recited the ancient prophecies passed down for many generations of Jews awaiting the Anointed One, their Redeemer.

Heli did not begin in Isaiah, but further back with Genesis 3 how God narrowed the line of Messiah with the passing generations. "From Adam, he chose Seth and his son Enosh, during whose lifetime people began to call upon the name of the Lord. Then God chose Noah, a righteous man in a wicked generation, and his son Shem." Moving on to Genesis 11, Heli recited the lineage of Shem, leading to Terah and Abram. Then his eyes lit up. "Children, God cut a covenant with Abram, later naming him Abraham, 'the father of many nations.' He was the father of all of the Jewish people. From him, God chose Jacob, and from Jacob, God chose Judah and blessed him, saying in Genesis 49, *'The scepter shall not depart from Judah, Nor the ruler's staff from between his feet...'* This was the establishment of the royal line that would produce King David. It is from this royal line that you have descended. Right now, the Jews are ruled by Herod. Right now, it looks like we are defeated. But someday, my children, one will arise as Messiah from the royal line of Judah.

"You can be proud to be in this family. No one would suspect that a poor family from Nazareth had such noble blood. But you do! I want you to know who you are! Messiah's birth has been foretold with many signposts so we will know who He is when He comes. God chose each son who would produce a son who would eventually become the royal line who would produce Messiah. Hold your heads high and watch for the signs of the coming Redeemer!"

Isaiah 11:1-5, 10

There shall come forth a shoot from the stump of Jesse, and a branch from his roots shall bear fruit. And the Spirit of the LORD shall rest upon him, the Spirit of wisdom and understanding, the Spirit of counsel and might, the Spirit of knowledge and the fear of the LORD. And his delight shall be in the fear of the LORD. He shall not judge by what his eyes see, or decide disputes by what his ears hear, but with righteousness he shall judge the poor, and decide with equity for the meek of the earth; and he shall strike the earth with the rod of his mouth, and with the breath of his lips he shall kill the wicked. Righteousness shall be the belt of his waist, and faithfulness the belt of his loins.

In that day the root of Jesse, who shall stand as a signal for the peoples—of him shall the nations inquire, and his resting place shall be glorious.

Preparing My Heart for Christmas

Pray for your children and grandchildren, even if they're not yet born. Ask God to establish a long line of faithful believers in all the generations that will come after you. Pray that your descendants will hunger and thirst for righteousness and have a willing heart to follow God's plan for their lives.

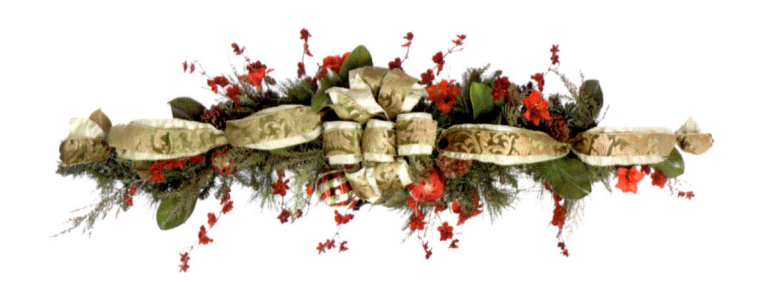

DECEMBER 7

The Virgin Birth Foretold

Lord, speak to me in a way I can understand Your voice and hear Your plans for me. I want to follow You. Please show me the way. I pray this in Jesus' name. Amen.

As her father read from Isaiah 7:14, Mary pondered his words. How could a virgin girl have a baby before she was married and slept with a man? That wasn't possible. But she knew God's Word to be true in all aspects, so as she thought about it, she began to wonder how that could happen and who that girl might be. Which Israeli girl would God choose as the mother of the Messiah who was to come?

It could be one of the wealthy, educated daughters of the priests in Jerusalem. Perhaps God would choose a virgin girl among the Levite's young women. Or maybe He would elect one from the long line of King David, the royal family line. She knew she was in that line. Her family could be traced all the way back to Adam through Abraham and King David. She drifted off to sleep that night, thinking about the prophecies concerning the One to come and wondering which young woman would be chosen to carry the king of all kings, the Messiah.

Prophecy:

"The scepter will not depart from Judah, nor the ruler's staff from between his feet, until he to whom it belongs shall come and the obedience of the nations shall be his." (Genesis 49:10)

Fulfillment:

[Jesus' genealogy.] "...the son of Amminadab, the son of Ram, the son of Hezron, the son of Perez, the son of Judah." (Luke 3:33)

Prophecy:

"When your [David] days are over and you rest with your ancestors, I will raise up your offspring to succeed you, your own flesh and blood, and I will establish his kingdom. He is the one who will build a house for my Name, and I will establish the throne of his kingdom forever."
(2 Samuel 7:12–13)

Fulfillment:

"This is the genealogy of Jesus the Messiah the son of David..."
(Matthew 1:1)

Prophecy:

"Therefore, the Lord himself will give you a sign: The virgin will conceive and give birth to a son, and will call him Immanuel." (Isaiah 7:14)

Fulfillment:

"The angel answered, "The Holy Spirit will come on you, and the power of the Most High will overshadow you. So the holy one to be born will be called the Son of God." (Luke 1:35)

Prophecy:

"But you, Bethlehem Ephrathah, though you are small among the clans of Judah, out of you will come for me one who will be ruler over Israel, whose origins are from of old, from ancient times." (Micah 5:2)

Fulfillment:

"When he had called together all the people's chief priests and teachers of the law, he asked them where the Messiah was to be born. 'In Bethlehem in Judea,' they replied, 'for this is what the prophet has written: "'But you, Bethlehem, in the land of Judah, are by no means least among the rulers of Judah; for out of you will come a ruler who will shepherd my people Israel.'" (Matthew 2:4–6)

Preparing My Heart for Christmas

Listen to Handel's "Messiah" on your devices and follow along with the scripture passages for a meaningful worship experience.

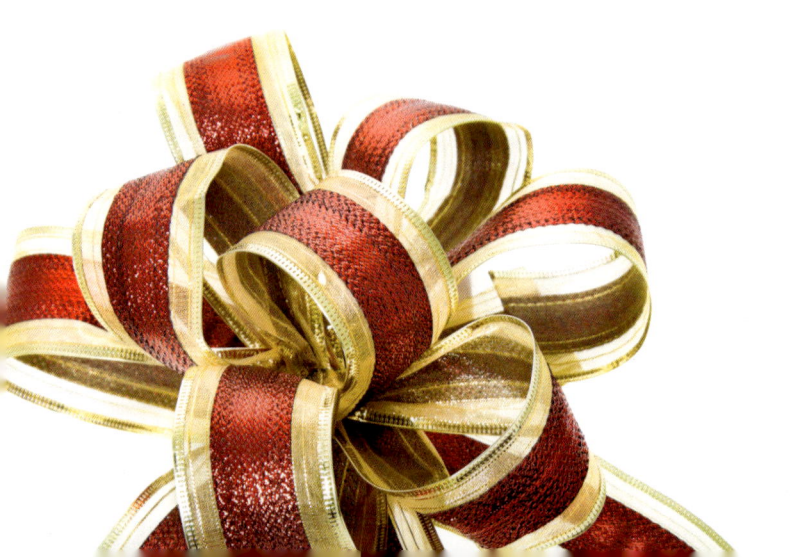

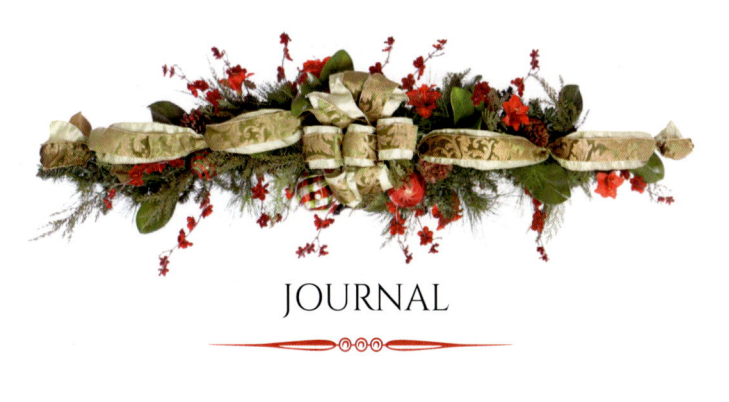

JOURNAL

_____

_____

_____

_____

_____

_____

_____

_____

_____

_____

_____

_____

_____

_____

_____

_____

_____

_____

_____

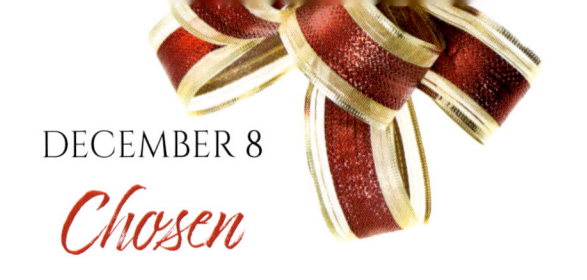

Chosen

Almighty God, thank You for loving me and choosing me before You created the world. I open my heart to receive Your great love. It is in Jesus' name, I pray. Amen.

Among Mary's people, it was common for cousins to marry. Israelite families stayed within their own tribes. The fathers of sons had a unique responsibility to find a proper bride for their sons, and Jacob felt the weight of this decision for Joseph, as they were of the descent of Kings David and Solomon in the line of men who inherited the right to sit on the throne of Israel. This young woman would be chosen not only for her beauty on the outside but for the beauty within, much like the bride of Isaac was chosen for him by Abraham's servant. Every father wanted to find a "Rebekah" for his son.

As Jacob, the father of Joseph, contemplated his choices from among the daughters of his relatives in Nazareth, one young girl stood out from the rest. She was young, yes, but she was stunningly beautiful. Her dove-like eyes, flowing, black curly hair, and lovely full lips often parted in a happy smile made Mary an object of attention from fathers eyeing her for their sons. The sons themselves saw Mary in a new light now that she had passed her fifteenth birthday. Mary didn't notice this heightened awareness from the men around her. That's what made her even more attractive.

Mary, the virgin daughter of Heli, also of the royal lineage of King David through his son Nathan, made a great choice for Joseph. While she had fun with her teenage friends, Mary exhibited a deeper, caring side. This lovely young woman often met the needs of homeless children and sick neighbors. She was just the kind of girl Jacob was seeking for Joseph.

Joseph, his eldest son, his heir, was strong and handsome, kind and good-hearted. Jacob and his wife took great pride in him and would find for him the perfect bride. She had to be very special to be worthy of their precious son.

Jacob felt it was time to secure the best bride in the village, for Joseph was now a man and already taking over much of the work of the family business in carpentry. He would take Joseph to speak to Mary's father this week.

Matthew 1:16, 18.

And Jacob the father of Joseph the husband of Mary, of whom Jesus was born, who is called Christ. Now the birth of Jesus Christ took place in this way. When his mother Mary had been betrothed to Joseph,

Luke 3:23.

Jesus, when he began his ministry, was about thirty years of age, being the son (as was supposed) of Joseph, the son of Heli,

---

Preparing My Heart for Christmas

The Christmas season can be overwhelming with all the decorating, baking, and gift-buying, and we can become stressed and anxious and take it out on our families. This year, take a moment to pause and write Philippians 4:6 on a note and put it on your bathroom mirror as a reminder during the weeks leading up to Christmas.

Simplify your gift-giving by giving experiences for the upcoming year. Give the gift of adventure (lessons for a new experience), the gift of time (mom-daughter or father-son night out or a special date with your mate), or the gift of service (childcare, house cleaning, or homemade meals).

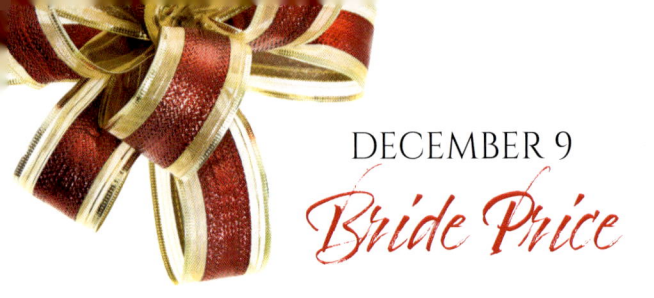

Bride Price

Lord Jesus, I thank You for sacrificing Your life for mine to pay for my sins. I receive Your gift of forgiveness humbly. I bow down to worship and honor You. In Your precious name I pray, Amen.

———⟨◦⟩———

Jacob called Joseph from the carpentry shop early that day. It was time to make a journey to the home of Mary to speak to her father. The two of them walked silently, side by side, contemplating the significance of this meeting. Joseph took a deep breath and stopped. Jacob turned to find out why. "Father, after today, if Mary's father will accept your choice to make her my bride, my life will never be the same."

Jacob smiled. "Son, if they accept our choice, Mary's father will set the bride price. Joseph, Mary is exceptional. Her father will require a high price to obtain her as your bride. We have many steps to complete before you can bring this young woman home. Let's take one step at a time. We'll see if Mary's father welcomes us and what he requires as a bride price for this special daughter. Prepare yourself. It will require something sacrificial."

They found Heli working outside the house and called to him. He knew what this was about the minute he saw them standing side by side, waiting for him to come down from the ladder. He had been both dreading and looking forward to this day. His beautiful Mary could not be kept at home much longer. The men of the village had been talking about her for months. He knew Joseph had taken a special interest in her and wasn't surprised to find him standing in his yard nervously kicking the sand. Joseph was a good and godly man. He was a bit older than Heli had envisioned for Mary, but a more mature man could handle life's challenges and he was of David's royal line. This was a good match. Heli would give his consent by setting the bride price.

It would be substantial. He would not allow his Mary to be obtained cheaply. He would set a high price so Joseph would know Mary's value and that marriage required sacrifice. It would also tell Mary her price was far above rubies.

He secretly hoped it would take Joseph a long time to collect the money to pay the price because he would keep his little girl close to home just a bit longer. How could he have known that in anticipation of his high price, Joseph had already sold his family's most precious possession—their Torah scroll. The Jewish law states that a family can sell their copy of the Torah to obtain a special bride for their son, and, in Mary's case, the price, although it cost them dearly, was well worth the sacrifice.

Joseph and his father could not have known that more than 30 years in the future from that moment, the young man who would call Joseph "father" would lay down his own life to pay the full price for His Bride. His Bride would not be a person but a people who accepted Him as the Messiah, the Son of God.

Genesis 34:12

"Ask me [Samson] for as great a bride price and gift as you will, and I will give whatever you say to me. Only give me the young woman to be my wife."

I Corinthians 6:20

...for you were bought with a price. So, glorify God in your body.

Preparing My Heart for Christmas

What sacrificial gift will you choose to give this Christmas season? Your generosity and thoughtfulness can make a meaningful impact on the lives of those you love.

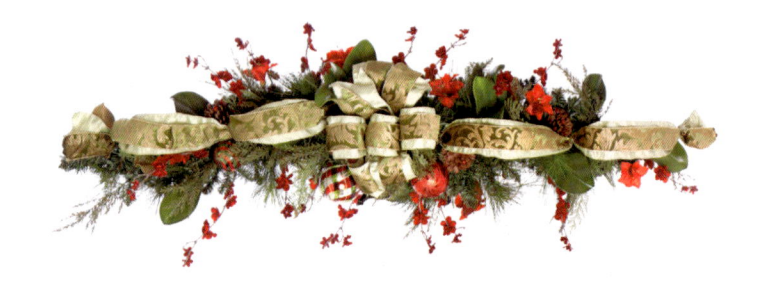

DECEMBER 10

The Betrothal

Lord, thank You that all of Your promises are "Yes" and "Amen."
Bless the name of Jesus and I pray this in Your name, Amen.

Joseph went to the door of Mary's home and took a deep breath. What if she refused to come to the door when he knocked? The agreement with her father would be invalid, and the marriage would not occur. But what if she did answer the door and open it wide for him? Did he dare to hope that this beautiful young virgin of Israel would open her heart to him on this night? His father stood in the road and cleared his throat, indicating it was time to knock. Joseph summoned his courage and knocked a little too loudly on the solid door. For a moment, he heard nothing. Oh no! She wasn't coming. She was refusing him. His mind went blank.

Just as he was turning to go, he heard the creak of the door as it slowly opened, and inside he saw her. His Mary. Big eyes shining, beautiful dark hair cascading around her lovely face, lips curved in a shy smile--this girl had his heart. He stammered out the customary question for any prospective groom in his position, "May I come in and dine with you, and you with me?" he said softly. She bowed, opened the door wider, and welcomed him with one word, "Come."

Joseph entered and joined Mary at a low table set with freshly made flatbread and a cup of sweet wine. They sat facing each other, hearts pounding, blushing but smiling, and Joseph quietly began to recite the blessing as they broke the bread. He looked into her eyes as he spoke the ancient words, "Blessed are you, Lord our God, Ruler of the Universe. May the sound of happiness and the sound of joy and the voice of the groom and the voice of the bride be heard in the cities of Judah and the streets of Jerusalem. Blessed are you, Lord, who makes the groom rejoice with the bride."

As he finished, they clasped hands and raised the single cup. First, Joseph, the initiator of their covenant, took a drink and then handed it to his bride. Mary brought it to her lips and closed her eyes as she drank, symbolizing that she was willing to drink from the same cup of life as her newly betrothed husband. They had sealed their permanent covenant agreement by taking this memorial meal. Their fathers joined them as witnesses for the next part while Joseph stood before Mary to read from his special scroll.

This was the ketubah, his sacred promise to provide her food and clothing and to bring forth heirs through her. Mary thought it strange that a young man had to promise to sleep with his bride because, of course, he wanted to do that! However, this ensured that a wife would have full provisions to be part of the community and could share in the covenant promises to Israel as she brought forth new sons and daughters of God's chosen people.

After their symbolic meal and the reading of the ketubah, Mary looked forward to the final part of the official betrothal ceremony. She stood now facing Joseph and watched as he pulled out a simple gold band and placed it on the index finger of her right hand. The moment this ring went on her finger, she was set apart only for him. She belonged to Joseph and would for the rest of their lives.

The holy, sacred, and legal steps had now been taken. They were betrothed, but in the eyes of the Jewish law, they were legally married. They would not come together as man and wife until after the official wedding, and that would be almost one year from now. But tonight, they sealed their covenant that wouldn't be broken.

Revelation 3:20

Behold, I stand at the door and knock. If anyone hears my voice and opens the door, I will come in to him and eat with him, and he with me.

Preparing My Heart for Christmas

This Christmas, make a conscious effort to fully open all the doors of your heart to Jesus. Let Him into the place where you are hurt and confused, and allow His love to penetrate to the deep places within. If you have not yet opened your heart for His salvation, confess your sins and receive His forgiveness. It is His greatest gift to you.

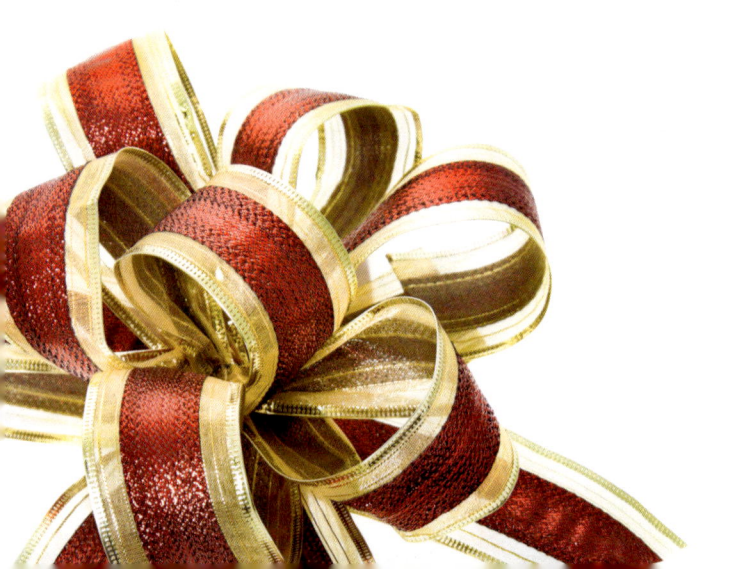

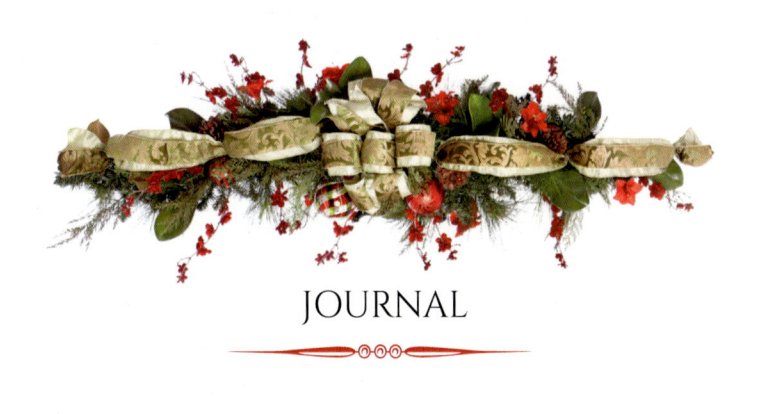

JOURNAL

_____

_____

_____

_____

_____

_____

_____

_____

_____

_____

_____

_____

_____

_____

_____

_____

_____

_____

_____

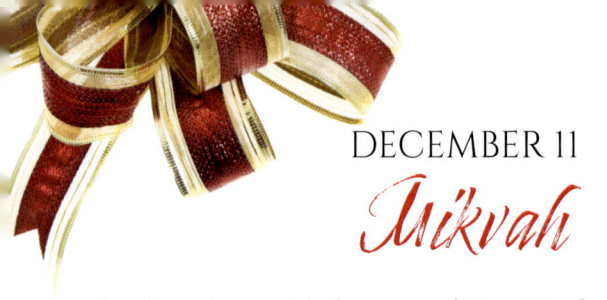

Mikvah

Lord, wash me with the water of Your Word, cleansing away wrong thoughts and renewing my mind. In Jesus' name. Amen.

———⟫◦✦◦⟪———

Mary began to prepare for her mikvah, the ritual cleansing of a Jewish bride before her wedding. It would help her internalize the big transition in her life to becoming a wife. As she entered the waters and later emerged, it symbolized leaving her singleness and entering married life.

For her mikvah, Mary first took a long bath in fresh water strewn with flower petals. While she bathed in seclusion, female friends and family members sang songs from the Scriptures. They teased her about becoming Joseph's wife and the many children they hoped she would have. Imagining life with Joseph, Mary smiled as she soaped her body in the warm water. After finishing her bath, Mary stood in the tub for the second part of the mikvah. A rainwater shower poured over the top of the privacy curtains as she scrubbed every inch of her body, starting with her hair and going down to her toes. She meticulously cleaned her ears and under her nails to ensure there was no speck of dirt anywhere on her body.

After thoroughly washing herself, Mary was wrapped in a cloth and led to the river's edge. Her mother watched with tears in her eyes as Mary walked into the shallow waters to immerse herself, symbolizing her transition into adulthood as a wife with new responsibilities. Proud of her faithful, obedient, and devout daughter, Martha prayed for God's blessings on Mary and her husband, Joseph, and for a future full of children. Mary took her first step into the cool Jordan River and slowly walked to the middle of the stream, where she could stand in water up to her chest. She took a deep breath and dipped down to completely immerse herself to the top strand of her hair, as commanded in the law.

As she arose, she prayed a blessing to honor God, who had created her and blessed her abundantly. Then she immersed again and rose to pronounce the second blessing, this time on her new husband and their marriage. She fully immersed for a third time and rose once more to bless their future children.

The moment the words came from her lips, she felt a slight tingle of electricity go through her body. It was as if God received that final prayer differently, and she wondered what children she would bear who would evoke such a response from the Almighty. She could feel the presence of God that day in a way she had never experienced before. She sensed that her marriage to Joseph was especially significant, although how, she couldn't imagine, as they were nobodies from an obscure village. She couldn't wait until the day he would come to claim her as his bride. They would walk in a joyous, torch-lit procession through the street at midnight with their friends and family to Joseph's home, where they would become man and wife. Her bridesmaids were prepared with oil in their lamps, and her dress was ready. How could she wait for the night Joseph would arrive with a shout to call her to come away with him?

> **Ephesians 5:25-27**
> *Husbands, love your wives, as Christ loved the church and gave himself up for her, that he might sanctify her, having cleansed her by the washing of water with the word, so that he might present the church to himself in splendor, without spot or wrinkle or any such thing, that she might be holy and without blemish.*

Preparing My Heart for Christmas

Today, love and respect your spouse to build a stronger bond during the Christmas season. Focus on strengthening your relationship by showing appreciation and kindness towards them with something simple like a warm hug, a simple compliment, and active listening when they speak.

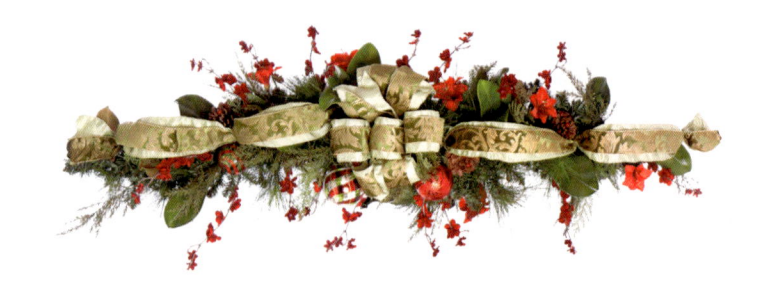

DECEMBER 12
The Angel

Father, I accept Your will for my life at any cost.
I choose what You have chosen for me.
I love You and pray this in the name of Jesus, Amen.

M ary's heart was full. She was daydreaming of her life with Joseph, having their children around her feet, cooking special meals for her family, and of evenings at the end of the day, curled up in his arms after the children were asleep. Those had been her dreams since she could remember. She hummed to herself as she went about the tasks her mother had assigned. Joseph, her betrothed, was preparing a place for them to spend their lives together. She would wait for him as long as it took. Someday, perhaps soon, he would come to claim her as his bride, his wife. She would leave her mother and father and be joined to him to become one flesh. They would build a God-fearing family and establish a strong home among the people of Israel.

She went outside to take in the wash when she heard a voice calling her. "Greetings, O favored one," he said. "What in the world?" she thought. "Who would say such a thing to me? Was he speaking to someone else? And who was this mysterious person or being or whatever it was? Was she imagining it?"

Then he spoke again, "Do not be afraid, Mary, for you have found favor with God. And behold, you will conceive in your womb and bear a son, and you shall call his name Jesus." Her heart skipped a beat. There was no doubt now. This was an angelic being from heaven. She was having trouble focusing on the words that followed his incredible news. Something about the baby being the Son of the Most High God and taking the throne of David.

Her heart was pounding, but somehow, she managed to ask a simple question. "How is this going to happen?" The angel explained what would take place in a way that reminded Mary of the creation of the world when God hovered over the waters and brought forth life. This is how it would be with her. With Mary. A simple girl from Nazareth. Nobody. And yet, chosen to be the mother of her Lord. Her response was equally simple: "Let it be done to me according to Your word."

Luke 1:26-38
In the sixth month the angel Gabriel was sent from God to a city of Galilee named Nazareth, to a virgin betrothed to a man whose name was Joseph, of the house of David. And the virgin's name was Mary. And he came to her and said, "Greetings, O favored one, the Lord is with you!" But she was greatly troubled at the saying, and tried to discern what sort of greeting this might be. And the angel said to her, "Do not be afraid, Mary, for you have found favor with God. And behold, you will conceive in your womb and bear a son, and you shall call his name Jesus. He will be great and will be called the Son of the Most High. And the Lord God will give to him the throne of his father David, and he will reign over the house of Jacob forever, and of his kingdom there will be no end."

And Mary said to the angel, "How will this be, since I am a virgin?" And the angel answered her, "The Holy Spirit will come upon you, and the power of the Most High will overshadow you; therefore the child to be born will be called holy—the Son of God. And behold, your relative Elizabeth in her old age has also conceived a son, and this is the sixth month with her who was called barren. For nothing will be impossible with God." And Mary said, "Behold, I am the servant of the Lord; let it be to me according to your word." And the angel departed from her.

Preparing My Heart for Christmas

God speaks in a way we can hear and understand Him. Make it a point today to be aware of His presence and listen for His voice.

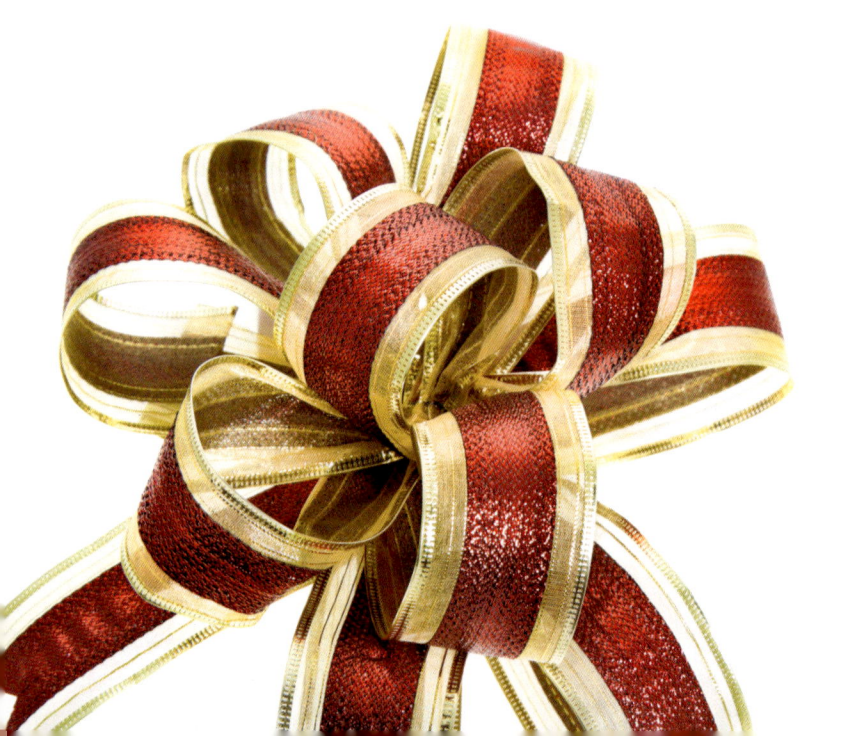

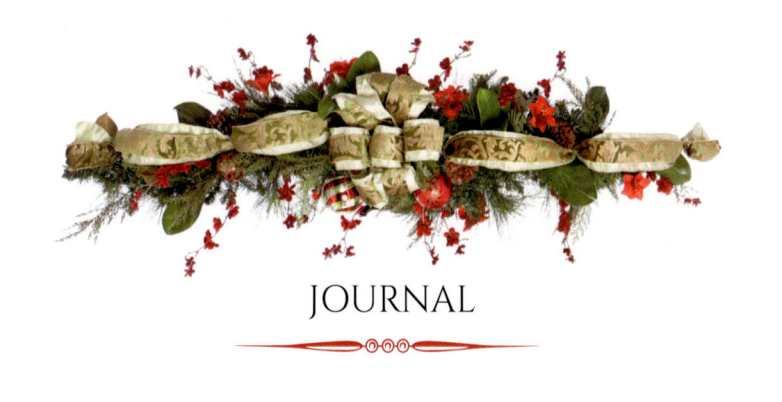

JOURNAL

Joseph

I bow before You, Father, and ask You to strengthen me with power through Your Spirit in my inner being so that Christ may dwell in my heart though faith. In Jesus' name, Amen.

Mary had to talk to Joseph. He was a man of God, a true worshipper. Joseph would understand. But how could he understand what she could not? It was so preposterous, so outlandish to think that she was chosen to bear the Son of God. It was unthinkable, but it was true. How could she make him understand that she had not been unfaithful to their betrothal vows? She was sure he would know she was telling the truth. But was she sure? How could she even start to explain the unexplainable?

Just then, she caught him out of the corner of her eye. He was delivering a beautiful table to their neighbors from his family's carpentry shop. She had to catch him as soon as he left the home before he could return to his family. She wanted to share the fantastic, terrifying, wondrous, and horrifying news with her betrothed. "Joseph!" she called from across the yard. He lifted his head to see her, and his face lit up in a smile that melted her heart. He was so happy, having just delivered a table that had taken weeks of painstaking work. He would have more time and money to work on their bridal chamber and new home. Just thinking about building the bridal chamber where they would spend their week-long honeymoon made him blush under his full beard. She surprised him with this unexpected but most welcomed visit.

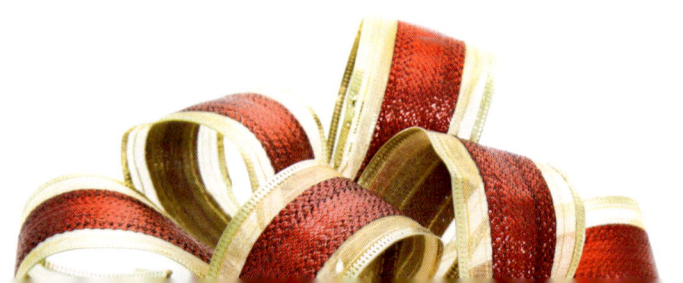

"Mary!" he answered, taking long strides to close the gap to where she stood. But as he drew nearer, he could already tell something was wrong; something had happened. She looked different, and he wanted to know exactly what had changed her. "Mary, are you all right? Your eyes, your face...something.... Mary, what is it?" She studied his face, trying to form the words that would either thrill or anger him. She began with, "Joseph, you need to sit down." His heart sank. It's never good when someone starts like that. "Joseph, I have something to tell you that will be hard to believe even though the prophets have foretold it. It will sound like I'm not telling the truth, but Joseph, I have been completely faithful to you. I have done nothing wrong." At those words, he braced himself. Was she going to tell him she was calling off the wedding and had decided to marry someone else? Why was she talking about her faithfulness? Had a man attacked her?

His eyes clouded as they looked deeply into hers, trying to comprehend the terrible news she was delivering. But she didn't continue the way he thought she would. She said, "Joseph, you and I have been chosen by God to bring the Messiah into the world." She stopped and let that sink in. "What are you talking about, Mary?" he stammered. "Joseph, I am going to have a baby." If she had stabbed him in the heart, it would not have ripped his soul as much as those words. "What??" he cried, "Mary, how could you? What have you DONE!"

She waited while he ranted and fumed, accused and interrogated, and finally crumpled in tears before her. She hadn't expected it to be this bad for him. She had accepted the angel's announcement, but it was different for Joseph. He was being asked to believe an angelic message second-hand, to believe the truth about Mary when all of the evidence pointed to her guilt, and to swallow his pride. He would surely be the laughing stock of Nazareth and would never, ever live down the shame of it all. He had been so careful with Mary, never crossing the line of respecting her and keeping his distance physically. He wanted nothing to spoil their wedding night. And now this.

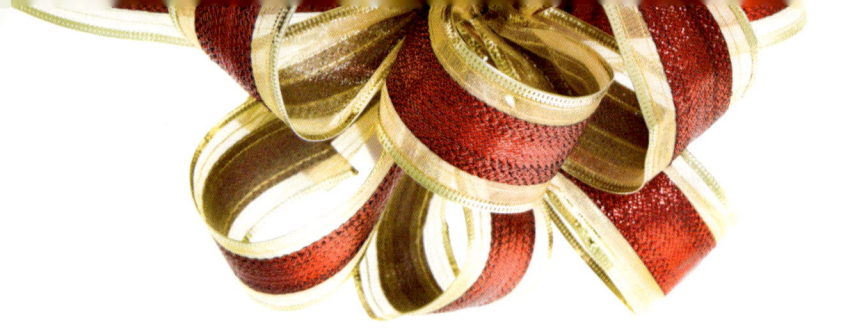

Betrayed, his rage turned to hurt, turned to doubt, turned to defeat. How could she? But she must have been attacked out in the field, and when she cried for help, no one was there to rescue her. Who would have dared molest his Mary? Joseph felt the urge to kill the man responsible.

But as he looked down at her upturned face, he saw only pure, sweet innocence. She was asking him to believe her incredible, shocking story. She was pregnant before their wedding—that was reality. To believe the message from an angel quoting from Isaiah was just too much to handle. Everyone knew the Messiah would be born to a virgin, but to believe it was his Mary, from Nazareth, was a stretch. He would have to sort out his feelings before sorting out his thoughts. He would search the Scriptures and cry out to Yahweh.

Matthew 1:18
Now the birth of Jesus Christ took place in this way. When his mother Mary had been betrothed to Joseph, before they came together, she was found to be with child from the Holy Spirit.

Preparing My Heart for Christmas

Use Psalm 119:105 as your prayer all day today.
"Your word is a lamp to my feet and a light to my path"

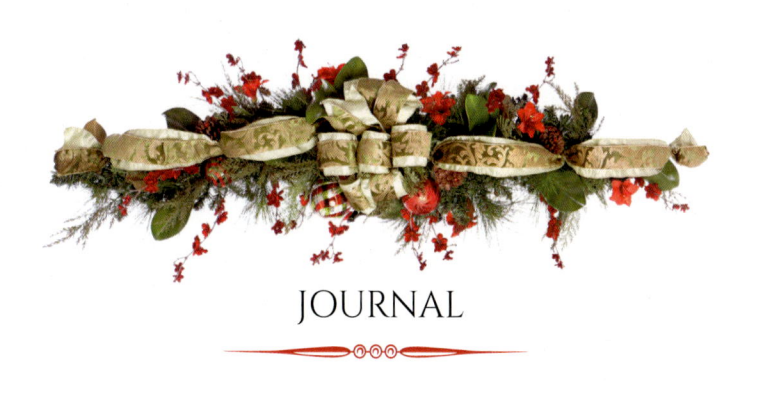

JOURNAL

_____

_____

_____

_____

_____

_____

_____

_____

_____

_____

_____

_____

_____

_____

_____

_____

_____

_____

_____

DECEMBER 14

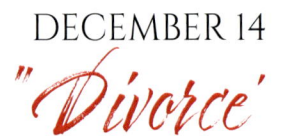

"Divorce"

Lord Jesus, when I am afraid, I will put my trust in You.
I pray this in Your name, Amen.

———◦◦◦◦———

She was gone. Mary had delivered her devastating news, standing silently, uttering not a word at his rebukes, accusations, and allegations. She packed up and left the city before dawn the next morning. Joseph was bereft without her. Moments before her announcement, he was ecstatic with joy to be her betrothed, and moments after the bombshell she dropped of the unplanned pregnancy, he was planning their divorce.

Jewish law mandated that their legal betrothal, signed and sealed by the elders and each other, was an iron-clad covenant agreement that must now be broken in court. He couldn't sleep, couldn't eat for the choking grief that blocked his heart from all rational thought.

Joseph knew the law in Deuteronomy 22:20, 21. *But if the thing is true, that evidence of virginity was not found in the young woman, then they shall bring out the young woman to the door of her father's house, and the men of her city shall stone her to death with stones, because she has done an outrageous thing in Israel by whoring in her father's house. So you shall purge the evil from your midst.*

But how could he turn his Mary over to the authorities and watch the stones break her body, sending her to an early death? How could he even consider such a thing? He was a God-fearing, law-abiding Jew who loved the Lord with all of his heart, mind, and soul. He knew God's Word was just, and this law was given to purify Israel. But what if—no, it seemed impossible—what if Mary weren't lying? That was ridiculous. Virgins don't have babies.

35

Just then, as he was turning the matter over and over in his mind, the Scriptures from the scroll of Isaiah surfaced in his memory. *"A virgin shall conceive and bear a son, and his name shall be called Immanuel. God with us."* His mind went back and forth, wanting to believe Mary, believe the prophecy, have faith in her, and then quickly take the opposing thought of her betrayal and sin. What should he do? What was the truth?

This preposterous situation had brought shame not only to Mary but also to him, and he didn't ask for this! If he divorced her, he would watch her die, and the grief of sentencing her to death would never leave him as long as he lived. But if he accepted her as his wife, then all of Nazareth would accuse him of taking her to his bed before the wedding. Joseph would bear the full brunt of incrimination because no one would believe Mary would have sinned that way unless he had forced her. He couldn't win! There was no way out of this mess she had gotten them into. "Oh, Mary!" he thought. "How could you do this to us? Lord, what am I to do? How am I to walk in the light in this dark situation? Perhaps I can find a way to divorce her but do it quietly and still save her. Oh, help me, Jehovah God." Distraught, he tossed and turned that night and finally fell into a fitful sleep.

Matthew 1:19
And her husband Joseph, being a just man and unwilling to put her to shame, resolved to divorce her quietly.

Preparing My Heart for Christmas

Before you make an important decision, take it to the Lord in prayer. Wait to act until you hear from Him through His Word, through the messages He speaks to you in prayer, and it is confirmed by godly mentors in your life.

Visit to Elizabeth

Lord Jesus, I trust You with all my heart, and I do not lean on my own
understanding. In all my ways, I acknowledge You and trust You to
direct my paths. I pray this in the name of Jesus, Amen.

———◦◦◦———

Mary's mind was reeling. Her time with the angel was so
powerful, and she knew his message to be completely
true. She had tried to explain to Joseph that she would
have a baby but had never slept with a man. Poor Joseph took it
hard. It was worse than she could have imagined. He said things to
her she never thought she would hear from this usually kind man.

She was stunned to silence, and after listening to his tirade, she
turned and left him standing there. She hurried home, shaken to
her core. This wasn't going as she thought. She had joyfully accepted
the angelic message, but now she had doubts. Joseph had brought
up the law against young women who committed fornication, and
the requirement of the law was death. What was he saying? Would
he really send her before the court to be tried, found guilty, and
sentenced to death for something she hadn't done? Now, she began
to doubt his love.

Even as those thoughts crowded her mind, she felt God's presence
calming her. She remembered the angel's first words, *"Do not be
afraid, Mary, for you have found favor with God."* She would trust
God in this moment of crisis. She didn't know what the future held,
but she knew the God who held the future. If God sent her a message
that began, *"Do not be afraid,"* He knew she would be tempted to
fear. She stopped and repeated a short prayer under her breath. "I
trust You. I trust You. I trust You."

A sudden thought came streaming into her mind as she made her way home. Now she remembered more of the message, *"Your relative Elizabeth, in her old age has also conceived a son, and this is the sixth month with her who was called barren."* Elizabeth will understand. I need to visit Zechariah and Elizabeth! God has not left me alone. He has given me a woman who will help me. I must go home and pack quickly.

Her parents looked at each other quizzically when she asked permission to go to Judea to visit her cousin, Elizabeth. She had never taken a journey that far by herself, but just as they were considering it, some relatives stopped by for a rest on their own journey to Judea. Yes, they would be happy for Mary to travel with them. They would take good care of her all the way to Elizabeth's home. They had heard from other relatives that Elizabeth was expecting Zechariah's child in her old age, and it would be good to see for themselves if this was true. They wanted to congratulate the elderly couple on God's great blessing. They would make room for Mary and tuck her in among their own children. She would be in good hands.

Her parents finally conceded that it would be good to send Mary to Elizabeth in this time of need. Perhaps Mary could help the elderly woman with household tasks as she prepared for her baby.

> **Luke 1:36-37, 39**
> *And behold, your relative Elizabeth in her old age has also conceived a son, and this is the sixth month with her who was called barren. For nothing will be impossible with God. In those days Mary arose and went with haste into the hill country, to a town in Judah...*

Preparing My Heart for Christmas

Befriend someone who needs you. Perhaps a neighbor or workmate needs a listening ear or a helping hand. Make that one of your gifts this Christmas.

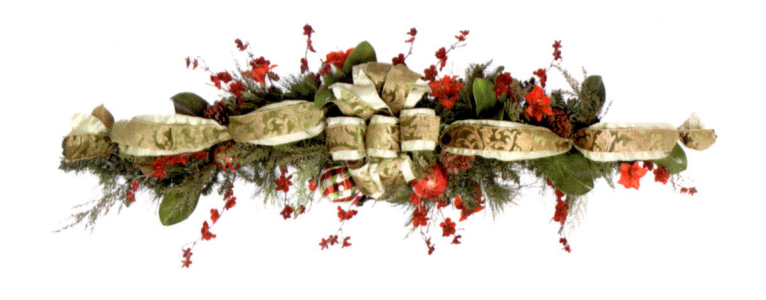

DECEMBER 16

Magnificat

Glorify the Lord with me, and let us exalt His name together.
Bless the holy name of Jesus, Amen.

⟨◦◦◦⟩

The minute Mary's feet crossed the threshold of Zechariah's home, she called to Elizabeth to announce her arrival. From the other room, Elizabeth cried out. Afraid something had happened, Mary rushed to find her cousin coming to meet her, cradling her big belly in her arms with tears streaming down her face. The older woman knelt on one knee before the bewildered Mary, exclaiming, *"Blessed are you among women, and blessed is the fruit of your womb! And why is this granted to me that the mother of my Lord should come to me?"* This was the confirmation that Mary needed to hear. This wise woman of God knew her secret without being told by human words. Elizabeth knew she was carrying the Messiah even now in his embryonic state.

What Elizabeth said next caused them both to burst out laughing. *"When the sound of your greeting came to my ears, the baby in my womb leaped for joy!"* Mary put her hand on Elizabeth's abdomen to feel that, indeed, the baby inside must be doing backflips. He was kicking up a storm, and while it brought a sharp pain to the older woman, Elizabeth was thrilled.

"He's been so quiet for days I was beginning to worry, but there is no problem with this strong son of mine. He knows even before his birth that his cousin has come from God. Mary, come sit down and tell me all about it while we have our tea and take some refreshments. You must be so weary from your journey. I have to hear the story. How did you know? How did it happen?"

The narrative tumbled out as Mary related all of the details for the first time. Joseph had been too upset to hear it all, and she dared not tell her parents until she had had time to absorb it all herself. They would never understand. With joy, Mary shared with Elizabeth the whole account from start to finish. Elizabeth drank in the glorious details and assured Mary that she would be greatly blessed for believing God's message through the angel. Mary's profound faith astounded Elizabeth. As the girl told her story, they both realized they were witnesses to a miracle of God for the ages. Mary's heart was bursting, and she cried out,

"My soul magnifies the Lord, and my spirit rejoices in God my Savior, for he has looked on the humble estate of his servant. For behold, from now on all generations will call me blessed; for he who is mighty has done great things for me, and holy is his name. And his mercy is for those who fear him from generation to generation. He has shown strength with his arm; he has scattered the proud in the thoughts of their hearts; he has brought down the mighty from their thrones and exalted those of humble estate; he has filled the hungry with good things, and the rich he has sent away empty. He has helped his servant Israel, in remembrance of his mercy, as he spoke to our fathers, to Abraham and to his offspring forever." (Luke 1:46-55)

The two women sat in silence and knew this to be a holy moment usually reserved for priests like Zechariah, who served in the temple. God Himself had been with them this afternoon, making His presence felt and understood. Having shared this divine encounter with the living God, they both were changed. Mary and Elizabeth would carry this moment with them until the day they died.

No one else could have understood what it was like for one to carry the prophet who would make way for the coming Messiah and the other to carry the Messiah Himself. It was more than anyone could take in. But these two had found in each other a sisterhood that sustained them through this glorious assignment. One very young and one past her prime, both carrying the future of Israel.

Preparing My Heart for Christmas

Give yourself the gift of being still and knowing that He is God. Find a place and time to quiet your heart and mind before the Lord. Just sit in silence in His presence.

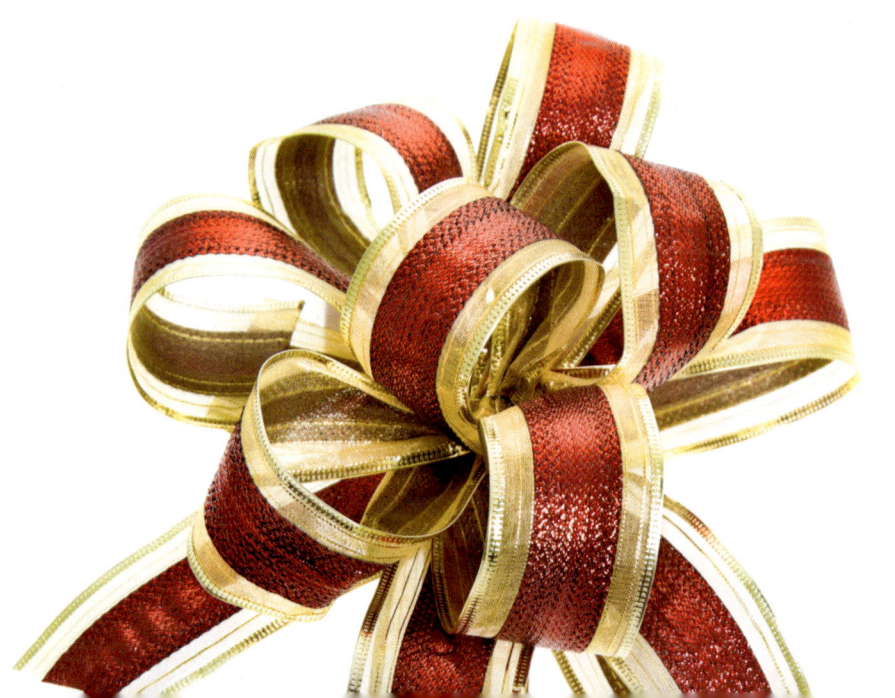

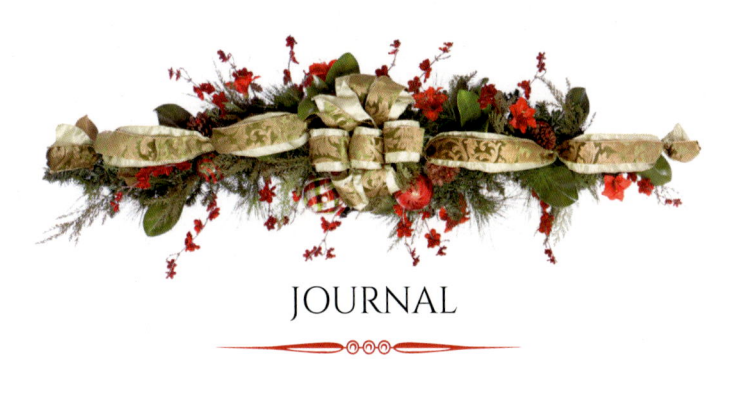

JOURNAL

_____

_____

_____

_____

_____

_____

_____

_____

_____

_____

_____

_____

_____

_____

_____

_____

_____

_____

_____

DECEMBER 17

First Trimester

Lord Jesus, Your Word says that I have been crucified with Christ, and I no longer live, but Christ lives in me. And the life I now live in the flesh, I live by faith in the Son of God, who loved me and gave himself for me. Help me to live this out in my life. In Jesus' name, Amen.

⟫◦◦◦◦

Mary awoke with an awful nausea. Her little room in Zechariah's home was near the entrance to the courtyard surrounding their home, and she rushed outside for air. She found a stone bench and sat down, holding her head. What was wrong with her? She didn't think she had eaten anything different. But wave after wave of sickness swept over her. She finally relieved her stomach of its contents and felt better...for a while. Then it started all over again.

When she could finally return to her room, she lay down, pale and drawn, and tried to go back to sleep. Elizabeth came to check on her when she didn't show up at the morning meal. As soon as she saw Mary, the older woman, now in her sixth month of pregnancy, knew exactly how Mary felt.

"It was like that for me for the first three months," Elizabeth said as she stroked Mary's brow. "It will pass. Just rest, drink a lot of water, and don't push yourself." "But Elizabeth, Mother and Father sent me here to help you, and here you are serving me!" Mary cried.

Elizabeth smiled and put her arm around Mary's slight shoulders. "You are carrying my Lord. Of course, I want to serve you. God brought you here to me during this first trimester because you need my help and understanding. You didn't need the disapproval of your family, the anger of Joseph, and the gossips of the town bearing down on you while you are already sick to your stomach.

It is God's mercy to bring you to me where you are safe, you are loved, and you have someone who understands morning sickness!"

Mary lay on her bed and fell asleep. This was unusual for her in the middle of the day, but she couldn't keep her eyes open. Elizabeth explained that while a mother's body is making a new life, her own bodily systems need to adjust, and for a while, she would feel very tired and out of sorts. Mary welcomed Elizabeth's directions to sleep when she was sleepy, to drink more water than she was accustomed to, and to let others do the heavy lifting in the house. She was carrying a precious treasure to be protected, even now.

Luke 1:56
And Mary remained with her about three months...

Preparing My Heart for Christmas

When you receive a calling from God, it may require you to make some significant sacrifices. It could involve giving up your personal desires, goals, or even your comfort zone. Take a moment to reflect on what God is asking of you and the personal cost it may entail. Remember that true obedience to God often involves self-denial, but the rewards of following Him are immeasurable. Are you willing to pay the price to follow Him?

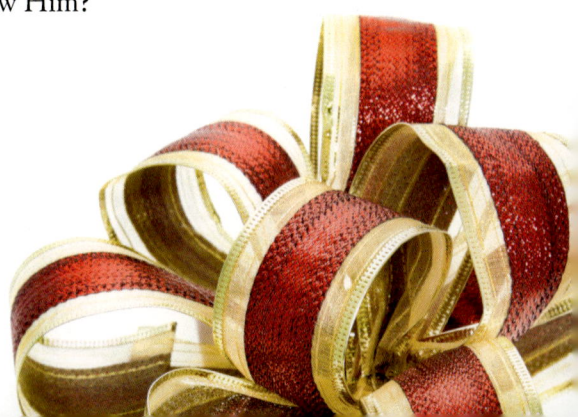

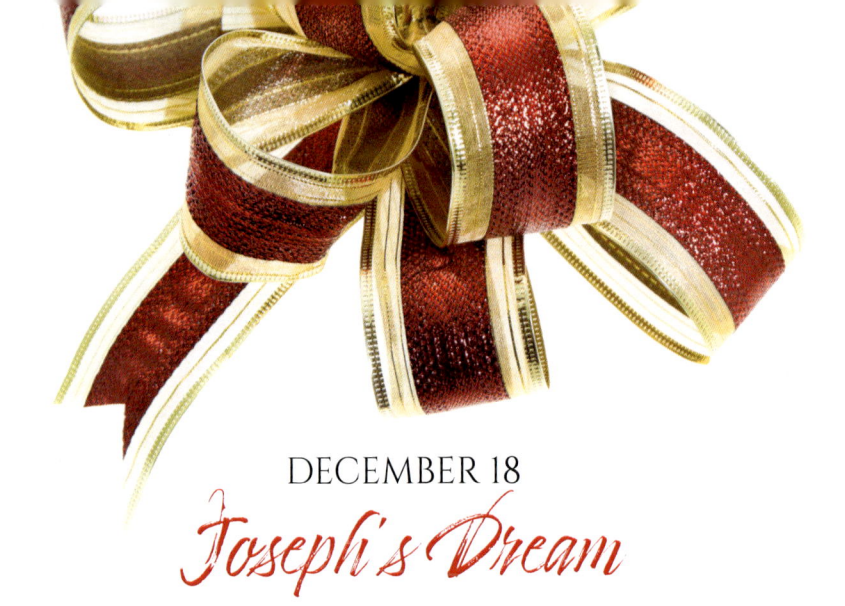

DECEMBER 18
Joseph's Dream

Lord, I choose to release fear and choose to trust You.
I ask that You enable me to be strong and courageous.
I pray this in Jesus' name, Amen.

Joseph had time to think with Mary away at her cousin Elizabeth's. Actually, he had too much time. He went over and over all of the possibilities for minimizing the damage for himself and Mary, but try as he might, he couldn't come up with a solution that satisfied his heart. He was miserable.

One night, after Mary had been gone for almost three months, Joseph fell into a deep sleep, and as his mind became still, he could finally dream. This dream was unlike any other. In it, Joseph was wide awake and was visited by an angel. When the angel began to speak, *"Joseph, son of David,"* he had Joseph's attention. Someone only referred to Joseph's royal lineage when the message was of utmost importance. The angel continued, *"Do not fear to take Mary as your wife."* At those words, Joseph felt the burden he had been carrying lift from his shoulders. It was his heart's desire to take Mary as his wife. He longed for her but was not sure it was right to take her into his home. Now, he was sure this message was from God. His heart was at peace.

There was more to the angelic message, *"For that which is conceived in her is from the Holy Spirit."* Somehow, now, that impossible truth seemed plausible. Of course, his Mary had remained pure, and of all of the maidens in Israel, no one was more worthy than she to be chosen to carry the Messiah. Yes, the Holy Spirit of God was bringing forth the one they had looked for so long. Tonight, in his dream, it all made sense.

"She will bear a son," the angel said. It seemed logical that the Messiah would be a man. *"And you shall call his name Jesus."* Well, that would be a hard one since no one in his family was called "Jesus." It would seem to implicate Mary's infidelity further if he didn't name the child after himself, but who was he to argue with an angel? If God wanted to name his son Jesus, so be it. And the final point of the angel's message was, *"for he will save his people from their sins."*

Joseph had more questions about that last part than any of the rest. How could Mary's baby save people from their sins? He had accepted God's Word up to this point, and he wasn't going to question Him now. "Yes, Lord. Let it all be done to Mary and me according to Your perfect plan. No one will understand. Our families will be enraged. The village will gossip for the rest of our lives. But, Lord, I have heard your call as clearly as Abraham heard your voice. I have seen your work as clearly as Moses saw the burning bush. I accept your plan for my life now at any cost. I will bear the shame of being reckless and impetuous and taking Mary before our wedding. I will sacrifice my honor as a law-abiding Jew and take the blemish on my name to see Your will be done on earth.

"I will take Mary, who is the purest but appears to be the most sinful young woman in the village, to be my lawfully wedded wife. And I will not touch her, even though she lies beside me, until she has delivered the Messiah. This, I promise."

Matthew 1:20-25

But as he considered these things, behold, an angel of the Lord appeared to him in a dream, saying, "Joseph, son of David, do not fear to take Mary as your wife, for that which is conceived in her is from the Holy Spirit. She will bear a son, and you shall call his name Jesus, for he will save his people from their sins." All this took place to fulfill what the Lord had spoken by the prophet: "Behold, the virgin shall conceive and bear a son, and they shall call his name Immanuel" (which means God with us). When Joseph woke from sleep, he did as the angel of the Lord commanded him: he took his wife but knew her not until she had given birth to a son. And he called his name Jesus.

Preparing My Heart for Christmas

Don't let fear steal your joy this season.
Follow God's call on your life courageously.

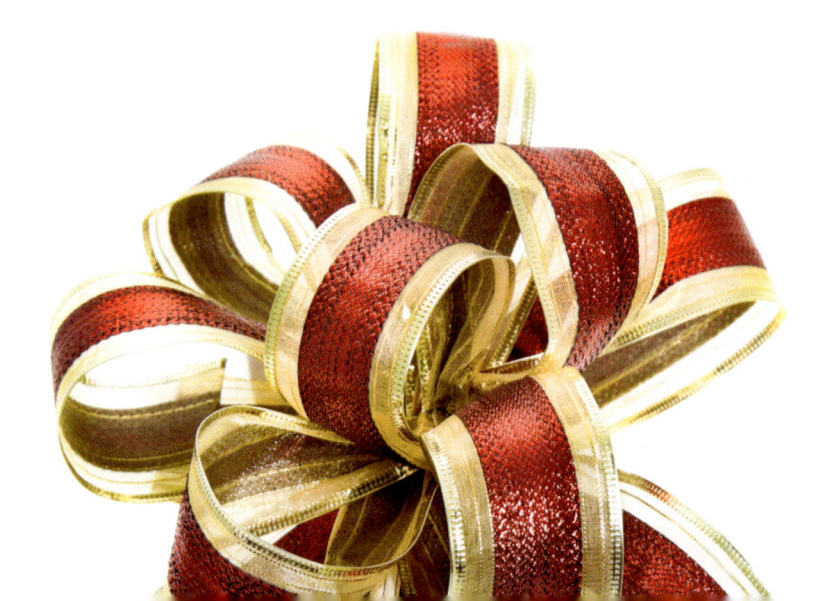

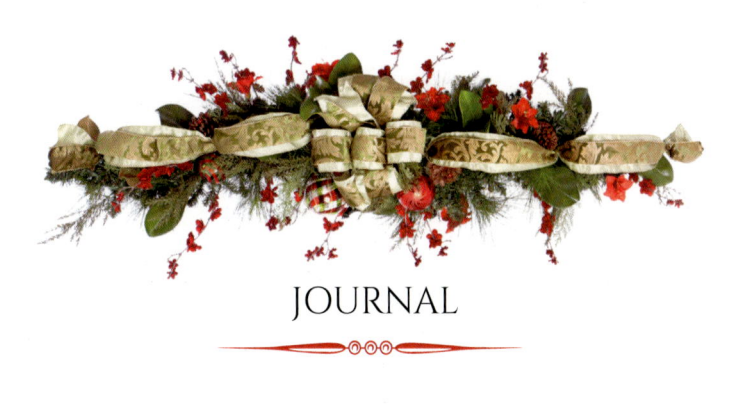

JOURNAL

_____

_____

_____

_____

_____

_____

_____

_____

_____

_____

_____

_____

_____

_____

_____

_____

_____

_____

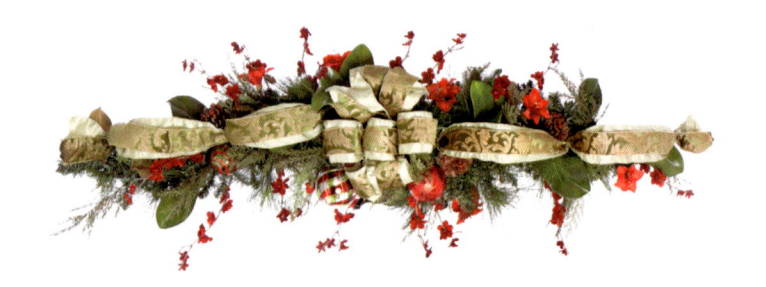

DECEMBER 19

Mary's Return

O come let us adore Him. O come let us adore Him,
O come let us adore Him, Christ the Lord. Amen.

———◦◦◦———

Mary traveled back to Nazareth with the same family that had brought her. Amazingly, they had let Elizabeth know they would be traveling back through and could take Mary home. It was time for Mary to face Joseph and her family, and it was time for Elizabeth to prepare for the birth of her baby.

The trip was difficult for Mary, and she was thankful to see her home come into view. She stepped off the cart and hurried into the house to find her mother. "Mother! I've missed you!" At the sound of her voice, Martha turned to see her long-lost daughter. She clasped Mary in her arms, and a shiver went down her spine. Mary was round right below her waist in the exact place Martha did not want to think about. Surely, she had just eaten good food at Zechariah's table and put on a bit of needed weight. It was good for her to fill out a bit. But the nagging thought wouldn't leave Martha's mind. What if? And the question lingered in her thoughts.

Mary's face had a new light. Martha supposed it was the joy of coming home and seeing her betrothed again. The wedding celebration would be nearer now, and Joseph might be letting them know of his plans any day to collect Mary in their triumphal procession to the bridal chamber. It was good Mary was home so they could prepare. But Martha couldn't shake the feeling that Mary was the same lovely and pure girl who left them three months ago, yet she was not the same. There was a distinct difference in her. What was it?

Mary had to see Joseph before she could begin to explain to her parents the wonderful news. Joseph had been so angry, so hurt, when she left him. How would she find him today? Was he still in a rage? Had it gotten better over time or worse? Well, she had to find out and must go now while she had the courage. She began walking to his house, and when she turned the corner, she almost ran into him.

When he heard that she had returned, Joseph quickly put away his tools, washed his face and hands, and set out to find her. They nearly collided and started laughing. "I didn't expect...." "I came to find...." Their words tumbled over each other. "You go first," Mary said politely. "Thank you, Mary. First, I must ask your forgiveness for how I spoke to you when you told me your news. You had seen an angel announcing the birth of the Messiah, and I treated you shamefully. I was caught by surprise, and it was a lot to take in, but I didn't believe you, and for that, I am so sorry. Please forgive me. Mary, I now believe and understand that God has called us to be the parents of His Son. It is incredible that God would entrust Him to us. But I realize that I may have lost my chance to be his earthly father by how I first responded. I want to know if you will still have me as your husband and the Baby's father."

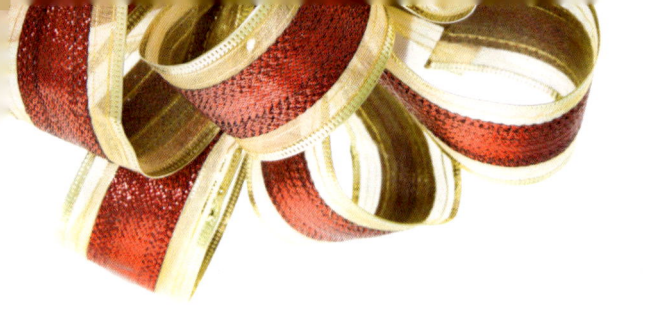

"Oh, Joseph, I cannot tell you how much I have prayed for you and how happy I am to hear that you, too, have accepted God's words to us through the angel," Mary said joyfully. Joseph grinned, "Well, I had an angel of my own who came to me in a dream and calmed all my fears. After that dream, I knew that this was God's plan for the two of us. It will be difficult, probably even more than we know, but I have surrendered my life into His hands and am willing to suffer shame for His sake." "Joseph, Joseph," Mary cried as he held her close. Even he could feel the little growing bump in her belly, and it made him more protective than ever of the Child who would be born of this virgin girl.

Luke 1:56
And Mary...returned to her home.

Preparing My Heart for Christmas

Most of us have had unwelcome surprises at Christmas. Our expectations about Christmas are rarely a reality, be it a gift not received or a visitor who could not come. Offer God your disappointments and ask Him to show you how to turn them into the best part of your celebration.

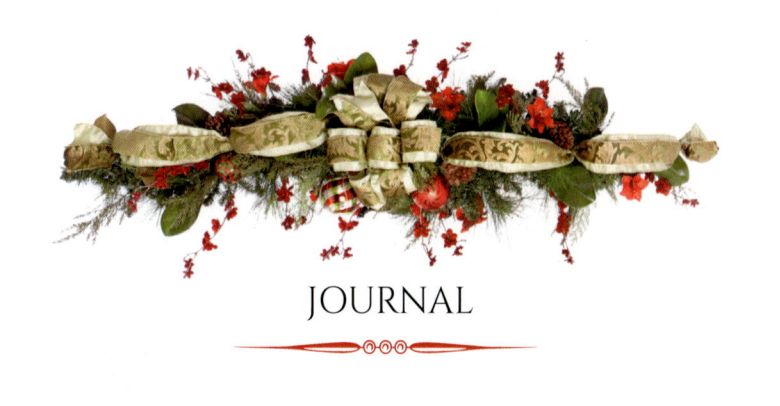

JOURNAL

_____

_____

_____

_____

_____

_____

_____

_____

_____

_____

_____

_____

_____

_____

_____

_____

_____

_____

DECEMBER 20
No Wedding

Heavenly Father, I know the plans You have for me: to prosper me and not to harm me, to give me hope and a future. Please give me the grace to trust Your plan. In Jesus' name, I pray, Amen.

W hen she returned home, Mary sat down with both of her parents, out of the earshot of her brothers and sisters, and quietly delivered her news. They were shocked, heartbroken, and disbelieving. Martha's nightmare was coming true. Mary was pregnant before the wedding. Mary informed them that Joseph would be coming for her tonight. There would be no happy procession in the streets, no lifting her up in the small cart to carry her to the wedding, no celebration meal with family and friends, and her white wedding garments would be packed away for her sisters' future weddings. She would never wear them. All of those dreams were gone.

She would quietly leave their home forever and live with Joseph, her husband, in the home he had prepared for them. They had trusted Joseph. And this is how he repaid them? He had spoiled their beautiful Mary. How could they ever forgive him? He had brought shame on their house.

As soon as Mary left the house with Joseph, her parents retired early to a fitful sleep. Where was God in all of this? All of the preparations and training of Mary to be a pure bride in Israel. What had happened? What had they done wrong? Why were they being punished? They held each other and cried long into the night.

Mary nodded to Joseph's mother, Esther, as she entered the home. The little rooms they were to live in were on the side of the house, and they had to go through the main house to reach them.

Esther cast a sideways glance at Mary and pursed her lips as she continued cooking. She didn't even stop to greet the young girl. This was not how she envisioned Joseph's wedding night. Sneaking his bride into the house under cover of darkness so the neighbors couldn't see was the exact opposite of how Esther had imagined this night. It should have been a community celebration, but here they were, cloaking their activities, hiding from the wagging tongues that would surely start tomorrow as the gossip about her Joseph and his Mary would spread through Nazareth.

When they finally reached the quiet of their room, Mary sat down on their bed and began to weep. This was going to be harder than she thought. She needed God's strength. Joseph sat beside her, put his arm around her, and began to pray, "Almighty God, You have chosen us for this assignment to bring Your Son into this world. It is too great for us. We don't know what to do, but our eyes are on You. Show us every step on this journey and how to follow Your plan. We trust You, and we love You, Lord. Amen."

Matthew 1:24, 25a
When Joseph woke from sleep, he did as the angel of the Lord commanded him: he took his wife but knew her not....

Preparing My Heart for Christmas

The holiday season is all about spreading love and joy, and what better way to do it than by reaching out to someone who could use some encouragement in their life? How about gathering your loved ones and preparing some thoughtful gifts for that special someone who might be feeling lonely this year? The best part of your Christmas may be the joy on their face when you present the gifts.

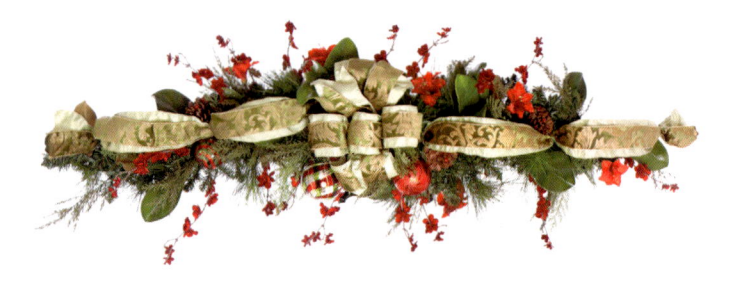

DECEMBER 21

Preparations

Lord, my Christmas preparations look nothing like those made to welcome you into this world. Let me see with clear perspective what is important and what is unnecessary. In Jesus' name, Amen.

<hr/>

The last six months had been the hardest of Mary's life. She was accustomed to being the delight of her community with approval from all, but she had endured loud whispers behind her back and outright scolding and shaming to her face. It was hard enough for a teenage mother to carry a baby with all the inconveniences of swelling feet, trips to relieve herself almost hourly, and shortness of breath as the baby grew. Even if you are carrying the Son of God, pregnancy is not easy.

She was completely dependent on Yahweh to get her through this. She and Joseph were on trial every day, always sentenced and punished by the rejection of the community of Nazareth. If only they could go somewhere to be anonymous to have this baby in peace. Just as she contemplated such a move, Joseph came home with news of a registration from the Roman government requiring them to take a journey. She was both elated and afraid.

"Mary, I don't have a choice," Joseph began. "I must leave our home in Nazareth and go down to Bethlehem as mandated by the decree from Caesar Augustus. The whole world must be registered in a census for taxation. This will be the first registration of this kind, and all of the officials, even Quirinius, the governor of Syria, are involved. Everyone is being mobilized to go to the birthplace of their ancestors. If I don't go, I will be imprisoned. I know this is a terrible time since you are so close to giving birth, but I want you to go with me. I don't want to leave you alone in Nazareth with the midwives who might not protect the child's life when you give birth. I am afraid for you. I have vowed to God to protect you and the baby with my life.

"It will take us at least a week or more if we cover the distance I have calculated for each day. This trip will be uphill and down on difficult roads; it may rain at this time of year and be cold at night. It won't be easy, but we will go as slowly as you need in your condition.

"I'll ask my mother and yours to bake bread for our journey, and we'll take skins of water. Mary, I'm sorry, but that is all we will have to eat for this trip, as we cannot burden the donkey with more. I'll also ask our mothers to prepare another bag for us in case the baby is born while we're away. I don't know what goes into such a bag, so please ask them what each item is and how we will use it if the time comes before we return home. I'm so sorry to put you through this."

Mary smiled at Joseph as he paced around their room. She could see his mind working through every detail. She was in good hands with this man who left nothing to chance. God had chosen the right man with the right skills to get her through God's plan.

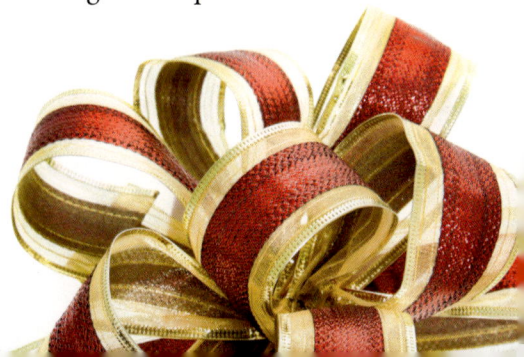

Mary needed to talk to her mother. Realizing that this journey to Bethlehem might mean she would not have her nearby for the birth required more preparation than anticipated. The prophets had foretold the birth of the Messiah in Bethlehem, so she was assured of God's plan, but no one had said how hard it would be on His mother!

Luke 2:1-5
In those days a decree went out from Caesar Augustus that all the world should be registered. This was the first registration when Quirinius was governor of Syria. And all went to be registered, each to his own town. And Joseph also went up from Galilee, from the town of Nazareth, to Judea, to the city of David, which is called Bethlehem, because he was of the house and lineage of David, to be registered with Mary, his betrothed, who was with child.

Preparing My Heart for Christmas

Read the Luke 2 Christmas story with your family tonight and discuss what it must have been like for Mary and Joseph to travel to Bethlehem.

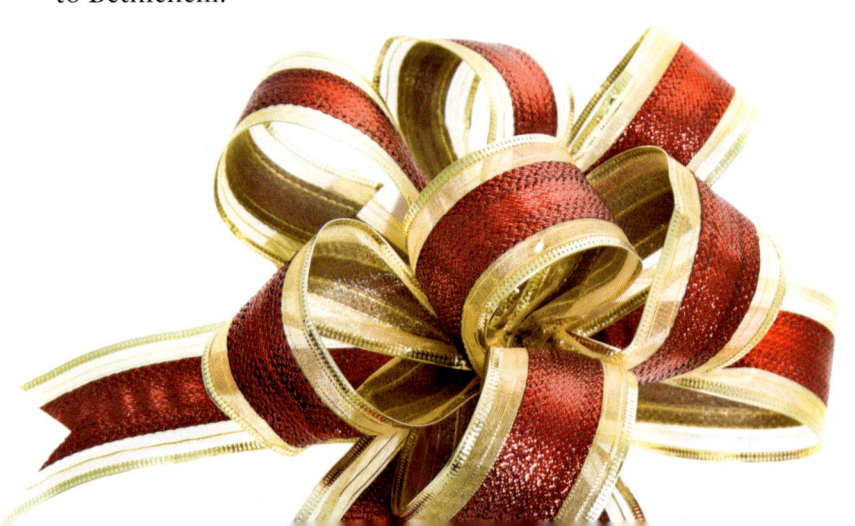

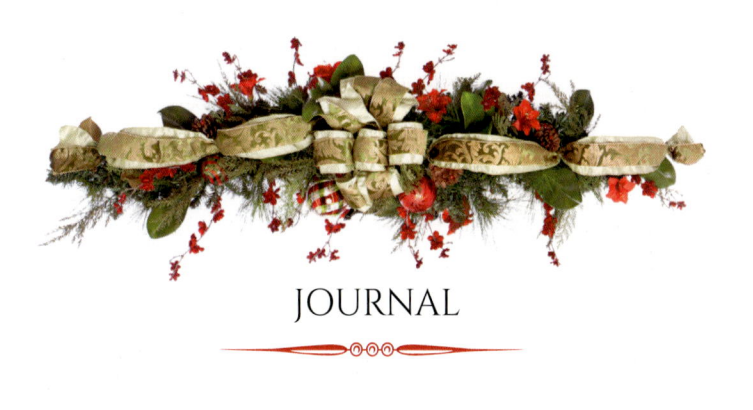

JOURNAL

—◇◉◉◉◇—

_____

_____

_____

_____

_____

_____

_____

_____

_____

_____

_____

_____

_____

_____

_____

_____

_____

_____

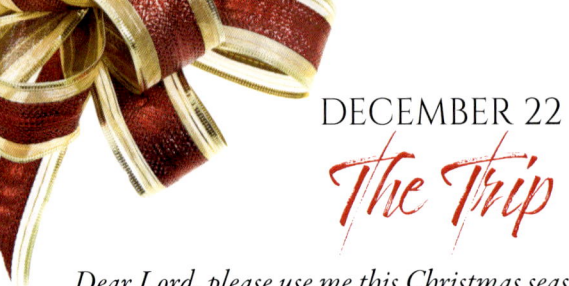

The Trip

Dear Lord, please use me this Christmas season to bring Your light into the lives of those around me. In Jesus' name, Amen.

———◦◦◦———

Mary sent up a prayer for God to have mercy on her and the Baby. They had only completed half of the journey, and traveling like this day after day, on the back of their little donkey, bumping over the stones in the road that jostled her, made her back ache, her stomach upset, and made Mary wonder if she could bear it. She knew that a trip of this kind all the way to Bethlehem so near to her time could bring the Baby sooner. The thought of going through that without her mother nearby to hold her hands and help her on the birthing stool made Mary shiver. "Lord, I don't think I can do this. Is this Your plan? Does it really have to be this hard?" And just as she was tempted to pity herself, the Scriptures her father had taught her from the prophet Micah surfaced in her memory. *"Bethlehem Ephrathah...out of you will come for me one who will be ruler over Israel."* (Micah 5:2)

She then heard the voice of God in her heart. "Mary, I will be with you, and I will never leave you. Joseph is taking you to the very place I have ordained for the birth of My Son. This is My will and My plan." From that moment, Mary settled on the back of the donkey and straightened her back. She smiled down at Joseph's worried face as he walked beside her. "It's all right, Joseph. God is with us, and this is His plan to bring His Son into the world in the city of Bethlehem. This decree is not of man but of God. Let's pray that God gives us the courage and strength for this journey."

Mary began to pray the words from the beginning of the scroll of Joshua when he was about to undertake a similar difficult journey to the holy land. "Lord, just as You were with Moses, we know You will be with us.

You will not leave us or forsake us. Help us to be strong and courageous for this journey. As we go, we will be careful to do according to all the laws that Moses commanded us. We will not turn from it to the right hand or to the left, that we may have good success wherever we go. This Book of the Law shall not depart from our mouths, but we will meditate on it day and night so that we may be careful to do according to all that is written in it. For then You will make our way prosperous, and then we will have good success. We are tempted to be afraid, Lord, as there are so many unknowns before us concerning the birth of this child. But Lord God, you have commanded us in Your word to be strong and courageous and not be frightened nor dismayed. We know that the Lord our God is with us wherever we go."

Joseph was amazed at this girl. She had faith that would move a mountain, and her faith encouraged his. He would protect her, care for her, and lay down his life for her and the Child she carried. He would take them to Bethlehem and trust the God of the Universe to accomplish His will through them.

Micah 5:2
But you, O Bethlehem Ephrathah, who are too little to be among the clans of Judah, from you shall come forth for me one who is to be ruler in Israel, whose coming forth is from of old, from ancient days.

Preparing My Heart for Christmas

As you wrap each gift this holiday season, take a few moments to offer a heartfelt prayer for the person it is intended for. Ask for God's blessings to be upon them and for His face to shine down upon them in the coming year. Pray that they will be showered with His grace and that their hearts will be filled with peace and contentment. May they feel the warmth of His love and the comfort of His guiding hand, no matter what challenges they may face.

DECEMBER 23

The Inn

*Father, thank You for supplying all of my needs according to Your riches
in glory in Christ Jesus. To You be the glory forever, Amen.*

---

nder normal circumstances, they would have expected to
stay in the spare bedroom of a relative, but Mary and Joseph
entered an overcrowded Bethlehem, and every family home
was bursting at the seams with relatives who had traveled from all
over Israel. News of Mary's pregnancy without the benefit of a
wedding had preceded them, and they found that they were not
welcome among their clan. No one was willing to make room for a
couple who had acted outside the law. After inquiring at house after
house, Joseph became desperate. His poor, exhausted Mary slumped
dangerously close to falling off the animal. Her face was drawn and
pale. He must find a place for her to lie down.

Joseph was forced to seek lodging at a primitive inn. The innkeeper
was rude and surly, hurling insults as he shouted that he had no
space, even on the floor. Business was booming, and he didn't need
these poor beggars from rural Nazareth with their country accents.
Just as he was about to slam the door in Joseph's face, the innkeeper's
wife saw Mary's condition. "Let them stay in the cave at the back of
the lot we use for the animals. We can get some money from them,
and no one else will be willing to stay there. Look at her. Have a
heart. At least there, they can get out of the cold." The innkeeper
glared back at the woman, knowing he would never hear the end of
it if he didn't listen to her. He gestured with a nod to the place they
could stay.

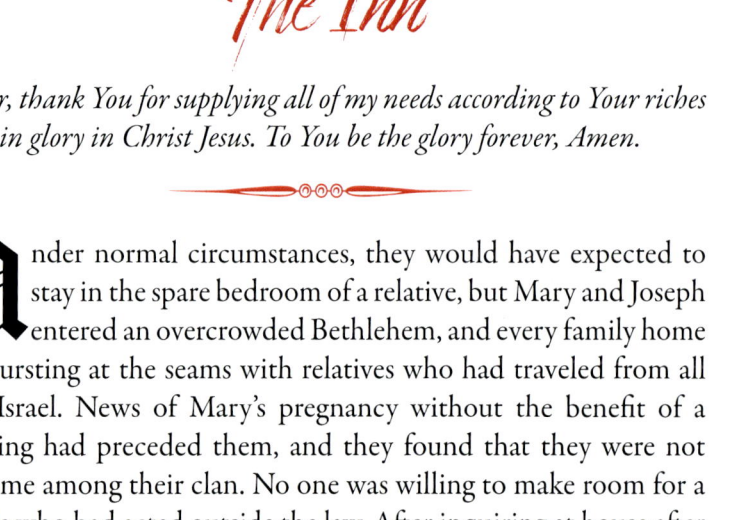

The cave-like stable was filled with donkeys from travelers staying at the inn, along with a few sheep the innkeeper kept there. The smell of dank and moldy straw, combined with animal manure, caused Mary's stomach to lurch. Joseph helped her off the donkey's back as she stretched her legs and rubbed her back. At least they were away from the crowds. She walked around to get feeling back into her tired body while Joseph cleaned out the dirty hay and unbound some clean bails stacked nearby. He unpacked the donkey's back and spread some blankets on fresh hay so Mary could lie down.

While she protested that she needed to help him set up their little campsite, she knew he was right. She did need to lie down. The trip had taken its toll. She would rest for a bit and then do her part. But within minutes, she was fast asleep, allowing her swollen body to completely relax for the first time in nine days and nights on the road. Joseph looked down on this teenage girl, and his love for her overwhelmed him. He got an extra blanket and covered her quietly to avoid disturbing the sleeping mother.

He created a makeshift campsite in the crude surroundings. How had they come to this? Couldn't he provide something better than a dirty, smelly stall? He chided himself for not realizing what it would be like when they arrived in Bethlehem, but it was too late for that thinking now. They would make the best of this situation. It might even be fun to camp out alone. It had been tense at home since he brought Mary home without a wedding ceremony. What a fuss his mother had made, and the accusations from his father still stung. But here, he and Mary could have peace and quiet, and after they registered tomorrow for the census, maybe they would stay in Bethlehem for a while. This could be a good thing if the baby held off for a few days.

The next morning, Mary had a burst of energy. She began creating a nest for them in the simple cave. Joseph marveled at her. She had endured a grueling trip, and yet, today, she was brimming with vitality. Where did she get this new vigor? She bustled around, bringing stones together in a circle around the fire just outside the mouth of the cave, and cooked some barley soup in one of the simple pots they had brought. They were both tired of stale bread and welcomed the smell of something fresh. Joseph let out a sigh of relief. Mary was fine. This was all going to work out better than he thought. He just wished there had been room in the inn.

Luke 2:7b
...because there was no place for them in the inn.

Preparing My Heart for Christmas

If you find yourself alone this Christmas,
lend someone around you a helping hand.

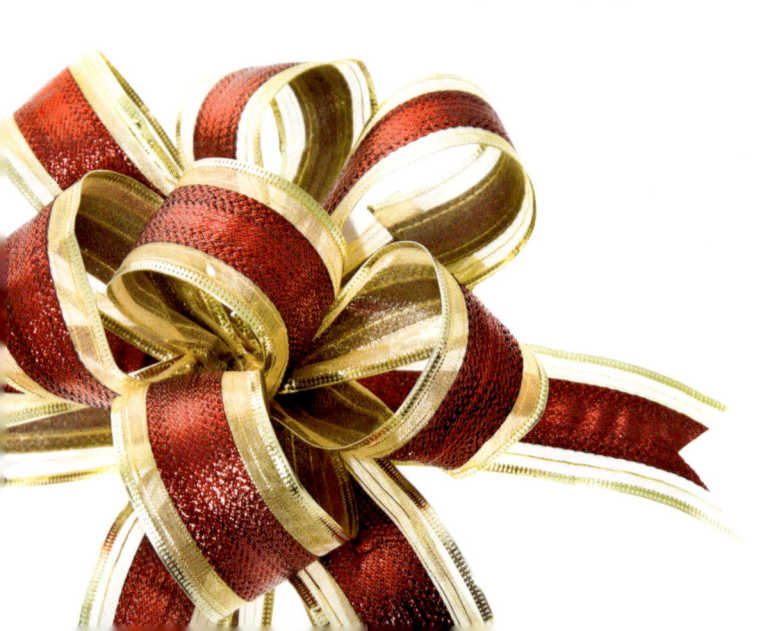

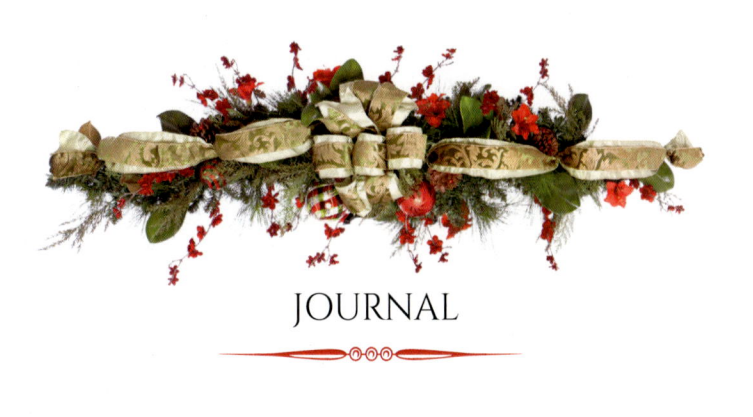

JOURNAL

DECEMBER 24

Labor

*Father God, breathe into me the breath of life this Christmas Eve.
I love and worship You, Jesus. In Your name, I pray, Amen.*

———◦◦◦———

Mary awoke in the night with a cry and felt her waters begin to flow onto the hay. "Joseph!" she cried. He woke with a start, "What! Is it time?" He was on his feet in seconds, pulling a heavy woolen cloak over his robes. "Mary, I'm going for help." "Please, Joseph, don't leave me here alone," she pled. "But, Mary, you need a woman who knows what she's doing. I'm going for a midwife. There has to be someone in Bethlehem who can help us." There was no stopping him—she could see that. "All right, but please hurry. I don't know how long this will take. I'm frightened, Joseph. I'm not sure this will be easy even though He is the Son of God." Joseph came to the side of their makeshift bed of blankets on the straw where she lay. "God is not going to leave us now. He is with us. While I don't understand it, this is His plan. This Child will be born, and you can do it. Sweetheart, it's going to be all right."

He even comforted himself with these words. Now, he just had to believe them. Secretly, he worried. Would he find help? Would it be in time? What if he had to deliver the baby himself? He had assisted farm animals in their time of birth, but a woman? His Mary? It was unthinkable. But he was ready to do whatever was necessary to bring the Son of God into this world. If he had to take on the role of a midwife to do it, so be it.

Joseph hurried out into the night. As she saw him go, Mary tried to make herself more comfortable. Her mother had told her that after the waters broke, the pains would soon follow. What would they be like? She sang to calm herself, even though she was afraid. A song of David came to mind, and she sang, "When I am afraid, I put my trust in you." She found that it helped put her mind at ease. Just then, the first of the pains began. They started deep in her back and came around to the front of her belly. It was unlike anything she had felt before. After a full minute of the tightening of her abdomen, it began to release.

The pains were erratic at first. Between contractions, she began making preparations for the baby. "Once He is born, where will I lay Him?" she mused. "I need to get Him off this dirty floor." She looked around inside the dark enclosure and found just the thing. "This little manger will work. He will be safe and warm if I put in fresh, clean hay and overlay it with the soft wool blankets I brought." Mary started laughing to herself and offered up a conversational prayer. "Lord, do you really want the Son of God, ruler of Judah, to be born in a stable and laid in a manger? This is the humblest, and dare I say, most humiliating place on earth for Him to enter earth's domain."

After she was satisfied that everything was ready for the baby, Mary looked through the bag of items her mother had prepared for this moment. There was a sharp, clean knife to cut the cord and a string to tie it off. There was salt to rub on the baby and swaddling clothes to wrap him in after the birth. She looked around to find something she could use as a birthing stool. Again, she found just what was needed, as if an angel had supplied this lonely cave as a birthing room. The small stool the innkeeper's wife used for milking was just the right height to lift her off the ground and put her in the right position to give birth.

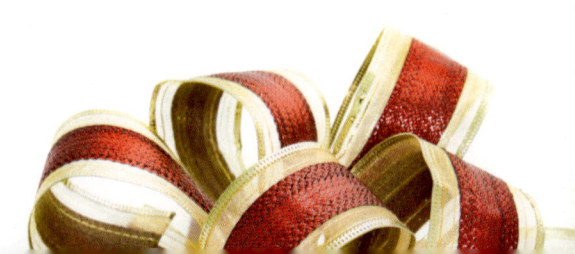

Her pains were now regular and much closer together. She could no longer walk about the cave but sat on the stool, waiting for Joseph to come. She heard footsteps nearing the cave's entrance. Joseph ran into the cave breathless and distraught from his frantic search for help. "Mary, I can't find anyone..." As he stepped near the light and saw Mary, he realized it was time. God had brought them to this moment and would supply everything they needed. Joseph took a deep breath and prayed. God would be with them, for He had assigned them to do what no other couple had been called to do. They were to be the parents of God's own Son.

Luke 2:6
And while they were there, the time came for her to give birth.

Preparing My Heart for Christmas

Make it a priority to attend services at your church on Christmas Eve or Christmas Day.

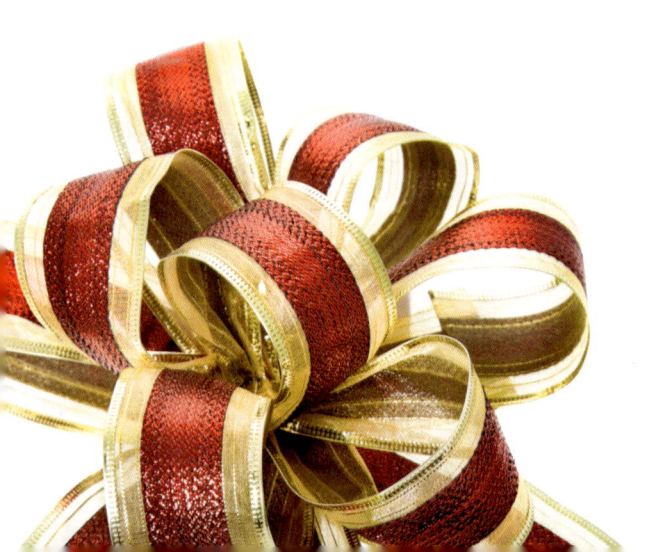

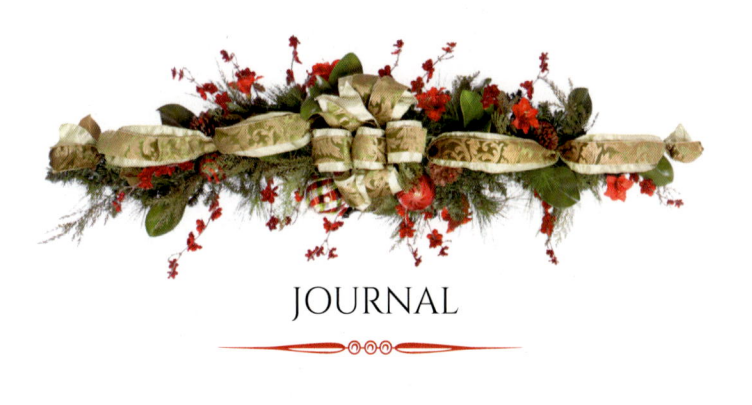

JOURNAL

_____

_____

_____

_____

_____

_____

_____

_____

_____

_____

_____

_____

_____

_____

_____

_____

_____

_____

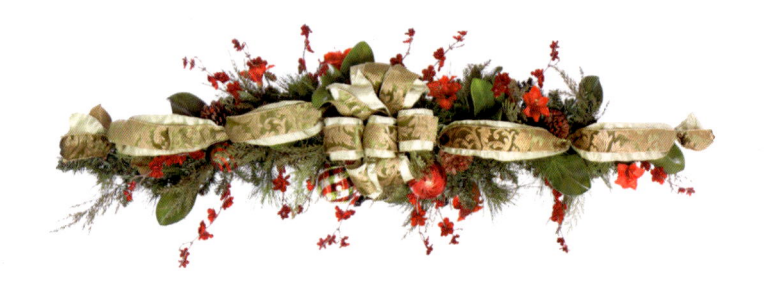

DECEMBER 25

A Time to Be Born

Thank you, Lord Jesus, for coming to earth as a Baby.
I worship and adore You, Lord. In Your name, I pray. Amen.

⤟◦◦◦⤞

It was time. Mary was in transition, and the birth was imminent. Joseph took her hand and allowed Mary to squeeze as hard as she needed. This was the final push, and he lent her strength to finish her task. "You're almost there, honey. Take a deep breath and push with all of your might." Mary gathered herself and bore down to bring forth her firstborn son.

As the baby boy emerged from Mary's body, Joseph caught him and placed him into her arms. He then cut the cord, tied it off, and, taking back the little one, rubbed his body with fine salt. He then wrapped Mary's son in the clean strips of cloth they had brought to swaddle Him. This boy was a beauty. Every feature of the dear little face was chiseled and exquisite. He was as healthy as any baby Joseph had seen. He was so proud of Mary. He busied himself, making her comfortable, and watched Mary wonder at her little child.

The baby had all ten fingers and tiny toes. His head was a beautiful shape, his hair was full and curly, and his legs were long and strong. His hands were unusually large. He would make a good carpenter in the family shop. But was this boy to be a carpenter?

Joseph remembered the angelic message: *"For he will save his people from their sins."* Surely, this child was the one they had waited for all their lives.

Joseph then remembered Isaiah's prophesy, *"Behold, the virgin shall conceive and bear a son, and they shall call his name Immanuel."* (Which means 'God with us.') In that cave of a stable, Mary and Joseph knew that God had truly come to earth that night. They cradled in their arms none other than God's Redeemer of all creation–the promised Messiah.

> **Luke 2:7-14 (KJV)**
>
> *And she gave birth to her firstborn son and wrapped him in swaddling cloths and laid him in a manger because there was no room for them in the inn. And there were in the same country shepherds abiding in the field, keeping watch over their flock by night. And, lo, the angel of the Lord came upon them, and the glory of the Lord shone round about them: and they were sore afraid.*
>
> *And the angel said unto them, Fear not: for, behold, I bring you good tidings of great joy, which shall be to all people. For unto you is born this day in the city of David a Saviour, which is Christ the Lord. And this shall be a sign unto you; Ye shall find the babe wrapped in swaddling clothes, lying in a manger. And suddenly there was with the angel a multitude of the heavenly host praising God, and saying, Glory to God in the highest, and on earth peace, good will toward men.*

Merry Christmas!

The Shepherds

Heavenly Father, I join with the angels in singing, "Glory to God in the highest!" Today, Lord, fill my heart with praise to adore You, to worship You, and to bow at Your feet. You alone deserve all the glory. In the holy name of Jesus, I pray, Amen.

It was the absolute worst job in the world. Keeping watch over some dumb sheep who would follow each other off a cliff if a shepherd weren't there to stop them. Benjamin and his friends were assigned the task of shepherding their families' sheep because, as the youngest sons in their tribes, they could do little else. Their elder brothers were busy with their fathers buying land, negotiating trades in the marketplace, and learning the family business. They would inherit the lion's share of everything their fathers owned. But the youngest sons had to divide the smaller inheritance between all of them. That would leave very little for the young men who now found themselves with some smelly sheep who always seemed to be wandering off. Tonight, the youth sat by their fires and dreamt of breaking free from the system that seemed so unfair.

That is, all except Benjamin. He was unlike the others. He marched to a different drummer. The thoughts that consumed him were not of attaining status and wealth, but his heart was filled with songs about Jehovah God and His promises. Just this week, he had composed a new song of worship to God about the coming Messiah. Benjamin could hardly keep it to himself. Every time he sang the song on the lyre while out in the field with the sheep, it made his heart soar and brought tears to his eyes. Even the chords in the song seemed anointed. The more he sang, the more he sensed that, somehow, God had revealed Himself to him and was preparing him for something. But what?

He was a nobody that even his own family didn't recognize as significant. He had nothing, he was nothing, he was going nowhere, but somehow, deep inside, he knew God had chosen him for something special. He couldn't imagine what it would be, but he knew it was just around the corner and coming closer every day. Then, suddenly, he understood. A beautiful, but blinding light covered the hillside and the most beautiful sound reached his ears.

Luke 2:8-14

And in the same region there were shepherds out in the field, keeping watch over their flock by night. And an angel of the Lord appeared to them, and the glory of the Lord shone around them, and they were filled with great fear. And the angel said to them, "Fear not, for behold, I bring you good news of great joy that will be for all the people. For unto you is born this day in the city of David a Savior, who is Christ the Lord. And this will be a sign for you: you will find a baby wrapped in swaddling cloths and lying in a manger." And suddenly there was with the angel a multitude of the heavenly host praising God and saying, "Glory to God in the highest, and on earth peace among those with whom he is pleased!"

Celebration of Christmas

As you begin to pack away the Christmas decorations, take a moment to sit back, relax, and delve into the heartwarming story of Luke 2 once again. Allow yourself to be fully immersed in the story's intricate details, reliving the wonder and beauty of the events that took place. Let the words of the story transport you to a place of hope and love. Cherish the true meaning of Emmanuel, God with us.

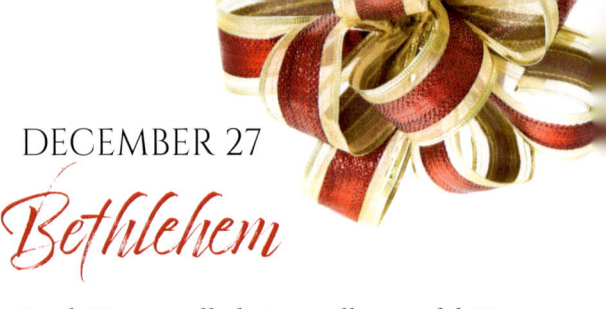

Bethlehem

I stand in awe of You, Lord. You are all glorious, all-powerful. Your name is above every name, and I bow at Your feet. Thank You for coming to earth to love us and to save us. Bless Your holy name, Amen.

———◦◦◦———

They were absolutely dumbfounded. The visitation from the angelic host, the glorious heavenly chorus, the sky lit up like a fire, and the amazing message would have been enough for a once-in-a-lifetime experience. But much more than all of these tangible things that assaulted their senses was the overwhelming sense of God's very presence.

It was more than the shepherds could have dreamed, asked, or imagined. The Most High chose the lowly young men to have a front-row seat on earth for a concert known only to heaven until then. No other living human beings had ever heard what they heard—without warning, their dreary night turned to glorious splendor. The curtain of heaven was pulled back, and God let them see and hear what was going on in the heavenlies that night. The angels couldn't contain their effervescent joy. It spilled out over the edge of heaven and fell to the earth right where the shepherds were watching their flocks. An obscure field became a stage where the rise and fall of a mighty chorus of angelic voices rumbled and shook the ground as the music soared.

These young shepherds were accomplished musicians, as music was the way to pass the long days and nights in the field, and small instruments could easily be carried along. The beautiful music they heard that night stunned them, made them weep, laugh, and bid them dance and sing along—every fiber of their being reverberated with the sound.

As soon as their minds cleared from the shock, they began to listen carefully to the lyrics of the songs that gave clarity to this visitation from God. This was none other than the birth announcement of a king. He was born that night in Bethlehem, and they were invited to go and worship Him.

They stumbled over each other as they hastily gathered their things and set out on a dead run for Bethlehem. As they had been told, they found the Baby King sleeping in a feeding trough, with His mother and her husband close by. No one but God would have thought to bring a King into the world in this way. After they left the precious scene, those young, uneducated shepherds became the first to share the gospel–the good news–He has come. God with us!

Luke 2:15-18

When the angels went away from them into heaven, the shepherds said to one another, "Let us go over to Bethlehem and see this thing that has happened, which the Lord has made known to us." And they went with haste and found Mary and Joseph, and the baby lying in a manger. And when they saw it, they made known the saying that had been told them concerning this child. And all who heard it wondered at what the shepherds told them.

Celebration of Christmas

In your preparations for the upcoming year, take some time to reflect on how you can share the great news of Christ's love. One way to do this is by joining a mission team at your church. Mission trips offer a unique opportunity to serve others and build meaningful connections with people from different backgrounds. You'll have the chance to witness firsthand the transformative power of Christ's love and be a part of something bigger than yourself. So, don't hesitate to explore this option and see where it takes you on your journey of faith.

Baby Dedication

Lord, I worship and adore You. Bless the name of Jesus. Your name is above every name in heaven and on earth. There is no one like You. Speak to me today in a way I can hear and understand You. Give me a heart to hear. In Jesus' name, Amen.

T he visit from the shepherds brought a new sensation to Mary. She realized at that moment that she would not be able to live out of the limelight from this moment on. Because of her baby, she and Joseph were no longer an anonymous Hebrew couple in a forgettable village. The whole world would know her Son, and consequently, they would most likely know her. For the quiet, shy young woman, it was another sacrifice she hadn't counted on.

She listened quietly as the shepherds spoke in hushed but excited tones of awe and wonder at the angel's announcement of her baby's birth. They described the night sky as filled with angelic beings singing the most glorious news. Joseph helped Mary calculate the time of the angels' appearance from their story and realized it was at the exact moment she had given birth. All that the shepherds spoke confirmed the wondrous things that had occurred over the past year–her visit from the angel Gabriel, her pregnancy and the quick trip to visit Elizabeth, her dubious homecoming, her parent's grief and unfounded disappointment in her, her hasty marriage without ceremony, the long months of waiting, the travel to Bethlehem in her final month, and the glorious birth of the Son of God. It was a lot to take in, and she needed time to ponder all of it.

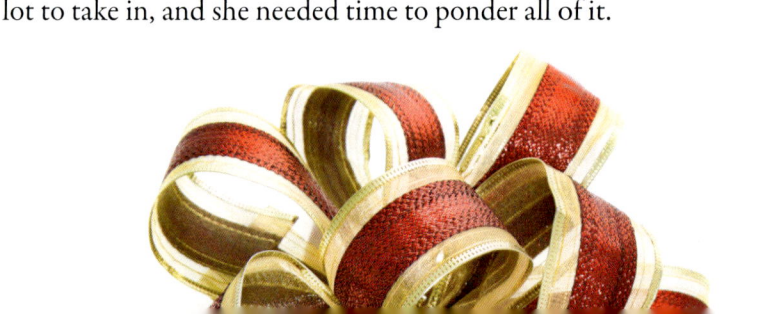

She was in heaven during the first week of Baby Jesus' life. Mary's whole existence was wrapped up in feeding Him, changing him, bathing Him, holding and rocking Him, singing to Him, and staring into His beautiful face. Joseph smiled as he watched the young girl he married become a mother overnight. She was a natural.

But soon, it would be the eighth day after His birth, and Joseph began making plans for the baby's circumcision. He located a rabbi in the local synagogue and set the time for the bris ceremony. The rabbi assumed this firstborn son would be named Joseph after his father, but Joseph quickly set him straight. "The Baby's name is Jesus." And under his breath, he whispered the angel's words, *"For he will save his people from their sins."*

Luke 2:19-21

But Mary treasured up all these things, pondering them in her heart. And the shepherds returned, glorifying and praising God for all they had heard and seen, as it had been told them. And at the end of eight days, when he was circumcised, he was called Jesus, the name given by the angel before he was conceived in the womb.

Matthew 1:21

She will bear a son, and you shall call his name Jesus, for he will save his people from their sins.

Celebration of Christmas

The week between Christmas and New Year's Day is often the quietest week of the year. Take advantage of the quiet to spend time alone with God to reflect on what you learned from Him over the past year and look forward to whatever He has for you in the future.

DECEMBER 29
The First Six Weeks

Lord Jesus, wash me in the water of Your Word. Purify me and cleanse my heart. I pray this in Jesus' name, Amen.

———◦⟁◦———

The law was specific and clear about the first six weeks of life with a new baby. Mary and Joseph knew and understood exactly what was expected of them after the birth of Jesus. When a baby boy is born, he is circumcised on the eighth day of life. His mother is "unclean" for forty days after his birth as her body sheds what nourished him in the womb. She must wait the full six weeks after the birth of her son to resume everyday life.

The parents would then bring the baby to the priest to present Him before the Lord. As a firstborn son, He was holy-- set apart for God's purpose. They were required to offer a burnt offering and a sin offering. Mary and Joseph had so little, but they would keep the law regarding the child. Joseph captured two young pigeons in the courtyard of the synagogue. They would be sacrificed to fulfill the burnt and sin offerings. They would lay down their lives for the Holy Child, Who would one day lay down His life for the world.

Leviticus 12:1-8
The Lord spoke to Moses, saying, "Speak to the people of Israel, saying, If a woman conceives and bears a male child, then she shall be unclean seven days. As at the time of her menstruation, she shall be unclean. And on the eighth day the flesh of his foreskin shall be circumcised. Then she shall continue for thirty-three days in the blood of her purifying. She shall not touch anything holy, nor come into the sanctuary, until the days of her purifying are completed."

"And when the days of her purifying are completed, whether for a son or for a daughter, she shall bring to the priest at the entrance of the tent of meeting a lamb a year old for a burnt offering, and a pigeon or a turtledove for a sin offering, and he shall offer it before the Lord and make atonement for her. Then she shall be clean from the flow of her blood. This is the law for her who bears a child, either male or female. And if she cannot afford a lamb, then she shall take two turtledoves or two pigeons, one for a burnt offering and the other for a sin offering. And the priest shall make atonement for her, and she shall be clean."

Luke 2:22-24

And when the time came for their purification according to the Law of Moses, they brought him up to Jerusalem to present him to the Lord (as it is written in the Law of the Lord, "Every male who first opens the womb shall be called holy to the Lord") and to offer a sacrifice according to what is said in the Law of the Lord, "a pair of turtledoves, or two young pigeons."

Celebration of Christmas

Begin preparing for the new year with a clean slate. Make right the things you have done wrong. Clear up miscommunications. Walk into the new year with a clean heart.

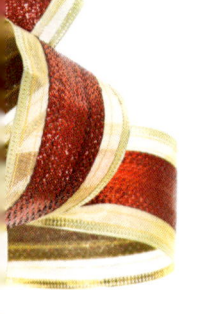

DECEMBER 30
The Temple

*Father God. I worship You. As this year comes to a close, open my eyes to
what You are calling me to do in the coming months.
I surrender my time into Your hands. In Jesus' name, Amen.*

———◈◉◈———

Mary and Joseph were both nervous and thrilled as they
packed the things they would need to present Baby Jesus
at the temple. They were country Galileans, and now
they would see the great city of Jerusalem and the beautiful, holy
temple Solomon had built.

They washed themselves and the Baby, tidied their shabby clothing as
best they could, and set out on their journey. Mary was thankful that
this time, as she sat on the back of the donkey, she had Jesus in her
arms instead of in her womb. She was able to enjoy traveling with her
little family as they made the momentous trip. This would be Jesus'
first visit to the temple, his first trip on the back of a donkey into
Jerusalem, but Mary sensed that it would certainly not be His last.

As the animal underneath her plodded along as Joseph led him,
Mary pondered what lay ahead for them today as they entered the
temple. How could anyone know Who she carried in through the
city's gates, up the road to the sacred temple? She was bringing the
King of Kings, but He would not sit on David's throne. She was
carrying the Prince of Peace, but the land was under harsh Roman
rule. The Word of God was in her arms as she rode past Pharisees
in their dark robes, discussing the minute details of the law. She
thought perhaps they would go completely unnoticed, an obscure
family with just another Hebrew baby boy coming for the ritual
purification that happened every day.

She looked up just in time to see a scholarly, elderly gentleman walking toward them with his arms outstretched to take the baby. Before she could react, he began to weep and pray over her Child.

Years later, she would relate to Dr. Luke the details of that day:

Luke 2:25-35

Now there was a man in Jerusalem, whose name was Simeon, and this man was righteous and devout, waiting for the consolation of Israel, and the Holy Spirit was upon him. And it had been revealed to him by the Holy Spirit that he would not see death before he had seen the Lord's Christ. And he came in the Spirit into the temple, and when the parents brought in the child Jesus, to do for him according to the custom of the Law, he took him up in his arms and blessed God and said, "Lord, now you are letting Your servant depart in peace, according to Your word; for my eyes have seen Your salvation that You have prepared in the presence of all peoples, a light for revelation to the Gentiles, and for glory to your people Israel."

And his father and his mother marveled at what was said about him. And Simeon blessed them and said to Mary, his mother, "Behold, this child is appointed for the fall and rising of many in Israel, and for a sign that is opposed (and a sword will pierce through your own soul also), so that thoughts from many hearts may be revealed."

Celebration of Christmas

Turn your eyes upon Jesus. Look full in His wonderful face.
And the things of earth will grow strangely dim,
in the light of His glory and grace.

The Redeemer

Bless the Lord, O my soul and all that is within me. Thank You for this past year, and I pray for Your will to be done in my life in the new year to come. In Jesus' name, I pray, Amen.

Mary was still processing the divine encounter with elderly Simeon. She had been startled but not surprised by his powerful prophesy over her Son. The words *"salvation for all peoples," "light for revelation for the Gentiles,"* and *"glory for the people of Israel,"* still rang in Mary's ears. The six-week-old Baby in her arms looked like every other Jewish baby in Israel—beautiful, dark curly hair, dark eyes, and olive skin. But she could also see what Simeon spoke of...a special light shone from within Him. He was so precious that her heart physically hurt from the overwhelming love she felt for Him.

She was looking down into His face, cooing and humming, and didn't hear the soft steps approaching across the smooth stones of the temple floor. She felt rather than saw Anna's presence as the old woman came to peer inside the blankets at her Son. When Mary looked up at the lovely, lined, and wrinkled face, she saw that same holy light emanating from Anna's countenance.

Anna was well-known to all who came to the temple. This eighty-four-year-old prophetess never left the sacred grounds. After only seven years of marriage, she had come to the temple as a young widow, desperate and empty, despairing and defeated, impoverished in every way. She had no one to turn to but the Lord. When she had thrown herself upon His mercy, He met her in that dark hour of need. She drank in the teaching of the Law and the Prophets that she could hear from the women's quarters.

She learned to pray the Word of God back to Him as her petition. She often fasted and interceded, and she longed for Messiah to come. For seventy-seven years, she had been exclusively the Bride of the Lord.

As she advanced in age, her time with the Lord became richer and sweeter than ever. One day, as she began to pray, God impressed on her heart that she would see the Messiah on this day. He instructed her to find a young couple bringing their very special baby for the purification ceremony of His mother. Just then, Anna saw Simeon leaving a little family. Tears were streaming down Simeon's face. He saw Anna approaching and nodded without a word. They both knew this was the day they had awaited all their lives.

Luke 2:36-40

And there was a prophetess, Anna, the daughter of Phanuel, of the tribe of Asher. She was advanced in years, having lived with her husband seven years from when she was a virgin, and then as a widow until she was eighty-four. She did not depart from the temple, worshiping with fasting and prayer night and day. And coming up at that very hour she began to give thanks to God and to speak of him to all who were waiting for the redemption of Jerusalem. And when they had performed everything according to the Law of the Lord, they returned into Galilee, to their own town of Nazareth. And the child grew and became strong, filled with wisdom. And the favor of God was upon him.

Celebration of the New Year

Spend part of your New Year's Eve in your prayer closet.
Ask God for a Scripture passage to pray over the coming year.